WATCH YOUR BACKYARD

THE CLANDESTINE THREAT OF EXTREMIST ISLAM & NARCOTERRORISM

BASED ON

"EL PLAN MAESTRO"
(The Master Plan)

Omar Bula Escobar

TABLE OF CONTENTS

INTRODUCTION

While the United States fights terror thousands of miles away from its homeland, distant foes like the Islamic Republic of Iran and Hezbollah have been stealthily lining up in Latin America with *"socialist"* governments and Transnational Organized Crime, with all but benign intentions. This sinister coalition, whose main purpose is to defy the U.S. from its *backyard,* is deeply involved in drug trafficking and crime, and has entered into shady deals which include the search for uranium and the exchange of nuclear technology.

Ignorance of the true extent of political globalization is emerging as one of the most harmful shortcomings of the U.S. and the West in the 21st century. A parochial perspective in political reasoning, invariably tied to partisan inclinations, has blurred a much more complex geopolitical *state of affairs* which few are able to recognize, and whose repercussions have momentous influence over U.S. and Europe's National Security.

"If all you have is a hammer, you tend to see every problem as a nail"

Abraham Maslow

In the words of China's Confucian philosopher *Xunzi*: *"In order to properly understand the big picture, everyone should fear becoming mentally clouded and obsessed with one small section of the truth."* And indeed, while *"the people"* of the United States confront each other vehemently to defend this or that presidential candidate, most are rendered sightless in regards to a common threat that concerns them all - irrespective of their political affiliations.

Prior to 9/11 and to recent Islamic State attacks in Paris and Brussels, U.S. and Europe's engagement in wars in the Middle East was considered a distant spectacle whose remote implications were of little concern to us. Today, we learn about Venezuela's ties with the Islamic Republic of Iran, about the growing presence of Islamic extremist groups in Latin America and their links to drug trafficking, or about nuclear technology transiting through the Panama Canal. However, we rarely take a step back to connect the dots in order to piece together the unsettling calamity that lies ahead. A series of competing and apparently disconnected events take place in front of our very eyes, gradually and unequivocally shaping the worst threat that the West has ever confronted. From the perspective of global geopolitics, the apparent disconnect between all these facts conceals a significant and disquieting correlation.

The world's geopolitical tectonic plates are still accommodating to a post-Cold War reality. Globalization has stirred alliances between countries and has prompted the emergence of new paradigms such as the ones posed by China as a new influential political and economic actor in the world stage, and by the clash between Islamic extremism and Western civilization.

Globalization has also emboldened Transnational Organized Crime. Previously improbable connections between drug trafficking, terrorism and crime have now gone global. Illicit trafficking networks in Latin America have associated with larger global terrorism networks in Africa and the Middle East, and Islamic terror organizations have profusely penetrated the US *backyard* - oftentimes with State support.

With its attention primarily focused on the Middle East, a distinct lack of understanding by the U.S. in regards to the new geopolitical dynamics unfolding south of its border has led to the end of the country's historical influence over its *backyard*. The result has been the spread of so called *"socialist"* governments throughout the region which have, in turn, allowed other countries such as the Islamic Republic of Iran, Russia and China, to fill the vacuum.

Capitalizing on U.S. distraction in regards to its *backyard*, *"socialist"* governments set up influential multinational structures and programs such as the **Foro de São Paulo (FSP)** and **XXI Century Socialism** which, over time, led to the emergence of *"narcopopulism"*[1], a fusion between States and powerful narcoterrorist organizations, in particular, Colombia's **FARC**. Meanwhile, FARC irrupted into the sphere of Transnational Organized Crime, linked up with

---

[1] "Narcopopulism" is further defined in Chapter 5

Islamic terrorist groups and is nowadays the planet's third richest terrorist organization.

The **Islamic Republic of Iran**, on its side, has been resolutely working to expand its influence in Latin America for more than a decade. Shared animosity towards the U.S. made of the new *"socialist"* governments in the region the ideal partners to further its agenda. With the help of Venezuela's late Hugo Chávez, the Islamic nation took advantage of U.S. absence to expand its terror network and opened the way for **Hezbollah** and other terrorist groups to penetrate the region. These groups established drug trafficking links with **FARC** and other narcoterrorist organizations, turning Latin America into a true *"terrorist nest."* Islamic extremist groups have spread out across the subcontinent expanding the reach of extremism, including the conversion of growing numbers of indigenous people by way of intense proselytism.

Watch Your Backyard focuses on the more intimidating upshot of these sinister alliances, one that is already simmering in the U.S. *backyard*, i.e. **the nuclear threat.** Based on *El Plan Maestro (The Master Plan)²*, a book I published towards the end of 2013, it describes an ominous international plot against the U.S. that has been underway for more than decade. The plot primarily involves Iran, *Bolivarian* countries, FARC and Islamic terrorist groups, and its main objective is to level the playing field with the U.S. by implanting nuclear capabilities on Latin American soil.

Within this menacing context, one particular event will most certainly constitute *the last nail in the coffin* for the burial of America's control over its *backyard,* and that is, Colombia's **Peace Talks** with **FARC.** We will see how the relevance of the *drug-tainted talks* goes well beyond Colombia's borders and the pivotal incidence these have over U.S. and European National Security. The book aims to show why international support for the ambiguous initiative is at dangerous odds with the global fight against terror.

While it only takes one disturbed fanatic to go through a Mexican tunnel with a powerful weapon to trigger unfathomable terror on U.S. soil, it is not difficult to imagine how a coalition of hostile nations linked to Transnational Organized Crime, and in full control of the US *backyard*, has the potential of expediting the plan. And like former U.S. Southern Command General John F. Kelly once said

---

² *EL PLAN MAESTRO (The Master Plan): IRAN - ALBA - FARC AND NUCLEAR TERROR,* was published in September 2013, in Spanish.

before U.S. Congress in regards to this particular threat, *"the word 'potential' is really important here."*

Watch Your Backyard's main goal is that of **cautioning** the American people and European nations with respect to a subdued, albeit harrowing threat, which too few recognize and far too many underestimate. As Union General *Lew Wallace*[3] once rightly stated: ***"In warning there is strength."***

---

[3] Lewis "Lew" Wallace (1827 – 1905) was an American lawyer, Union general in the American Civil War, governor of the New Mexico Territory.

CHAPTER 1

UNDERGROUND GLOBALIZATION

I.   GEOPOLITIC'S TECTONIC MOVEMENTS

The nineties laid the geopolitical foundations and generated the new paradigms which challenge most of the world today. After almost half a century of confrontation between the West and the Soviet Union, the fall of the Berlin Wall in 1989 shook the tectonic plates of global geopolitics. The blunt partition between capitalism and communism quickly vanished, forcing nations to reposition themselves within a new confusing and volatile international geopolitical reality.

During that same period, the U.S. enjoyed significant economic growth and relative prosperity. However, it also manifestly failed to assert its new position as the new global world power. In the meantime, Europe was too busy trying to make some sense out of its convoluted political union to assert its own. As a result, the assumption of a *"unipolar"* world with the U.S. and Europe in the lead rapidly diluted and as the world entered into the 21st century, a more *"multipolar"* world emerged, in which countries such as China, Russia, India and Brazil played the balancing act. And while the West *"rested in its laurels"* in terms of its relocation in the post-Cold War era, its foes did not hesitate to reorganize and capitalize on a growing and widespread *anti-Western* sentiment.

The September 11, 2001, attacks on U.S. soil constituted the first discernable milestone of the antagonism that has prevailed since the beginning of the 20th century, the one that opposes the West to radical Islam. In the Middle-East, enhanced animosity against Western nations led to the appearance of new extremist groups such as the abominable Islamic State, better known as *ISIS/ISIL* or *Daesch*[4]. In Latin America, taking advantage of the US's *"hands off"* approach to its *backyard*, authoritarian *Narcopopulist* governments led by Hugo Chávez filled the void and managed to thrive throughout the region. Acting under the ideological cover **XXI Century Socialism** and amid a growing gap between the rich and the poor, populist regimes were able to flourish, sustained by an unprecedented increase in world oil prices and sponsored by unholy alliances with Transnational Organized Crime. In turn, Chávez laid a red carpet for Islamic extremism to penetrate the region, closing ranks with the Islamic republic of Iran and facilitating the growth of Hezbollah's presence across Latin America. Furthermore, shared hostility against America's *"imperialistic"* policies resulted in disturbing and previously unthinkable transatlantic *anti-US* alliances.

II.   THE SEWERS OF GLOBALIZATION

As any new global phenomenon that breaks into the political, economic, social and cultural *status-quo*, globalization has been the subject of great controversy in terms of its *pros* and *cons*. Some praise its contribution to the global integration of international markets, increased international competition, lower production costs and the spread of global technology. Others, however, criticize the promotion of greater inequality between developed and developing countries and the exclusion of the lower segments of the population, which hardly have access to its benefits. In any case, a much less attractive face of globalization has been unfolding practically unhindered beyond these considerations: the globalization of crime.

Globalization has emboldened **Transnational Organized Crime (TOC)**, in terms of size, operational capacity and wealth. Criminal networks have taken advantage of the increased mobility of goods, services and people across borders - and have exploited the unprecedented interconnection of financial markets to further their illicit goals. Capitalizing on rapid technological changes, these have converted into much more sophisticated ventures and have expanded their global outreach. Moises Naim, former director of *Foreign Policy* magazine calls this *"the dark side of globalization"* and, indeed, crime has gone global. Transnational Organized Crime now counts upon extraordinary riches

---

[4] Daesh: Arabic name of the Islamic State: al-Dawla al-Islamiyah fi al-Iraq wa al-Sham

and power, capable of destabilizing governments, disrupting economies and enabling the spread of terrorism around the globe.

In Latin America, globalization's dark side grew concomitantly with an unprecedented expansion of the drug trafficking industry. The vast resources generated by the drugs and the criminal underworld represent today an increasingly significant share of the economies of the region. These have contributed to the intensification of the endemic scourge of corruption which has profoundly penetrated both the public and the private spheres in most countries in the region. By the same token, billions in public resources destined to economic and social development have been squandered.

III. TRANSNATIONAL ORGANIZED CRIME (TOC)

Transnational Organized Crime constitutes one of the most disturbing drawbacks of globalization and represents one of the most important threats to national and international security in the 21st century. While the world tries to adapt to a highly complex geopolitical reality, TOC toils stealthily and incessantly in the sewers of the underworld to further its criminal intent across the globe. Its primary criminal activities include drugs & arms trafficking, money laundering, illegal mining and contraband - even though it is also involved in more sinister ones such as human trafficking and human organ trafficking. According to the United Nations Office on Drugs and Crimes (UNODC) 2010 report, global criminal proceeds of TOC amounted to around 3.6 percent of the world's gross domestic products combined, or some US $ 2.1 trillion per year.

Major drug trafficking and other international criminal groups make use the world's finest legal, financial and logistics experts to run their business. These have also adopted the latest technological innovations to perpetrate their criminal acts. Sonars, radars, electronic coding and infrared systems - and even semi-submersibles, are part of their arsenal, to mention only a few[5]. The latest addition to TOC's array of lucrative illicit activities is that of *cybercrime,* which according to experts yields some US $ 100 billion annually.

But beyond TOC's potential to generate crime and acts of terror, its ever expanding tentacles are also having increasing impact over governance and democracies throughout the globe. State institutions, the military, intelligence and security services are being infiltrated, while members of government and high-level business executives are absorbed into the scheme (be it through intimidation or corruption). TOC influences legislation and controls the Media in order to generate the required political and economic conditions for its

---

[5] FARC has invested millions of dollars in the development of disposable submarines which are able to transport 8 tons of cargo more than 1,000 miles undersea.

criminal activities to thrive. This has led to the birth of 21st Century *Narco-States*, in which government and crime blend into one sole entity and essentially constitute systemic components of governance; two good examples are Venezuela and Guinea-Bissau (see box).

IV. DRUG TRAFFICKING: THE COLOSSUS OF THE SOUTH

"Drug trafficking is Latin America's atomic bomb'

Carlos Lehder

These were the words of Carlos Lehder in the late seventies, the first major Colombian drug kingpin ever extradited to the U.S. His prediction tangibly depicts well today's reality.

Admittedly, the war against drugs has failed. Despite the investment of billions of dollars and the loss of tens of thousands of lives, drug trafficking remains the most profitable crime in the world today. Its colossal size turns it into a truly monstrous industry which keeps national economies afloat and which has significant influence over the course of national and international geopolitics. In the context of the 2008 global financial crisis, UNODC warned that money from drug trafficking was even being used to prevent bankruptcies in the international financial and banking sectors.

According to the *Financial Times*[6], most commercial products around the globe experienced significant price increases over the past decades, with two noteworthy exceptions: heroin and cocaine. In real terms, heroin and cocaine are cheaper today than they were twenty years ago. The U.S. and Europe retain the top spot on the global consumption podium and a thriving market in both sides of the Atlantic evidences the defeat in the global fight against drugs. According to experts, while consumption in the U.S. has stabilized, Europe has

---

[6] Financial Times *"The 'Great Game' of Colombia's peace process."* John P. Rathbone / 05/09/2012

been witnessing an increasing demand for drugs and an unprecedented outburst of cocaine consumption.

Latin America has been the epicenter of drug production and trafficking for several decades. However, as a direct consequence of the failure to beat the scourge, the region is nowadays literally *submerged* in drugs. This extraordinary expansion has been led by Colombia's FARC, which has extended its reach to virtually every corner of the South American subcontinent, and by the Mexican Cartels, which have taken control of Caribbean and Central America drug trafficking routes to North America. Heroin, cocaine and methamphetamines are only some of the drugs that make up the arsenal of increasing powerful drug cartels and generate billions of dollars in revenue. According to UN sources, annual profits from illicit drug trade amount to a staggering US $ 322 billion a year.

The consequences of endemic drug trafficking are frightful. Narcoterrorism, defined as *"terrorism financed by profits from illegal drug trafficking"*, has become Latin America's tormentor. FARC's death toll alone adds up to more than 220,000 deaths and, like that of the Mexican cartels, its cruelty and ruthlessness is unnamable. Aside from breeding crime and violence *(Latin America occupies the highest ranks of insecurity and crime in the world)*, it also generates widespread corruption, causes permanent damage to public health and has calamitous and extensive impact on the environment.

GUINEA-BISSAU: THE ARCHETYPICAL NARCO-STATE

Guinea-Bissau is a former Portuguese colony in West Africa with 1.6 million inhabitants. The country has a huge external debt and has relied heavily on international aid to combat high levels of poverty. Since it gained independence in 1974 the African nation has been the subject of numerous military coups. In the late nineties it suffered a bloody civil war which left thousands of victims.

For the UN, Guinea-Bissau "is the worst Narco-State of the African continent. In the words of a DEA senior official "people at the highest level [in Guinea-Bissau] are involved in drug trafficking... in other African countries government officials are undoubtedly part of the problem; in Guinea-Bissau, the government itself is the problem." The country's last coup in 2009 was widely attributed to the involvement of the highest levels of government and the military in cocaine trafficking. In the aftermath of the coup drug trafficking figures soared and the number of aircraft coming from South America increased drastically. Most of these aircraft were sent by Colombia's FARC from Venezuela.

Regrettably, the problem is getting worse, as Latin American support for terrorism is increasingly benefiting from direct state support and judicial impunity.

ORGANIZATIONAL TRANSFORMATION

Among the most distressing developments in the ambit of Latin American drug trafficking during the past decades is the organizational evolution and transformation of 20th century rebel groups into criminal organizations. For *leftist* guerilla groups such as Colombia's FARC and Peru's Shining Path, the end of the Cold War translated into the loss of their main *"communist"* funding sources. In order to fill the funding gap, these groups got increasingly involved in the different stages of drug production and trafficking and gradually transformed into powerful full-fledged drug cartels. Today, FARC is responsible for at least 60% of Colombia's cocaine production and has grown to be the world's third richest terrorist organization (*Forbes, December 2014).*

The US Drug Enforcement Agency (DEA) defines narcoterrorism as the "participation of groups or associated individuals in taxing, providing security for, otherwise aiding or abetting drug trafficking endeavors in an effort to further, or fund, terrorist activities."

V. UNLIKELY ALLIANCES

As in any business, interests converge, joint ventures are agreed upon and outsourcing provides for its expansion - and the business of global crime is not the exception. Transnational criminal coalitions which cover practically the entire planet have been forged, enabling criminal groups to boost their capabilities and to expand their geographical reach. Amongst the most disturbing of these alliances is the *"terrorism & crime"* connection. Terrorist groups are increasingly associating with international drug trafficking organizations and powerful mafia groups in order to share logistics and expertise and to facilitate obscure international financial transactions.

A sinister international network in the realm of global criminal underworld has been created. Colombia's FARC and Islamic terrorist groups such as Al Qaeda and Hezbollah are involved in drugs & weapons trafficking across the Atlantic; Mexican Cartels work in close partnership with the Russian Mafia, and Italy's Calabrese Mafia teams up with FARC and Nigerian organized crime.

Perhaps the most revealing of these unholy alliances was staged by the Mexican "Zetas" cartel and Iranian regime agents in October 2011, when US authorities uncovered a plot to assassinate Saudi ambassador Adel al-Jubeir in Washington D.C. Reportedly, five of the terrorists involved in the plot were members of Iran's Quds Force High Command, a unit of the Iranian Revolutionary Guard. It is in this context that Gen. John Kelly, commander of U.S. Southern Command, warned US lawmakers in March 2012 that extremists were radicalizing converts and other Muslims in Latin America and that the Islamic State could take advantage of trafficking organizations in the region to infiltrate the United States.

"One must also note the growing convergence of terrorist organizations with criminal cartels like the drug trade to finance their activities. Such cooperative activities will only make terrorism and criminal cartels more dangerous and effective."

The Joint Operating Environment, 2008

VI. THE AFRICA CONNECTION: THE NARCO-JIHAD

In the light of the emergence of the notorious Mexican drug cartels and as a result of the saturation of the Caribbean and Central American routes to smuggle drugs into the U.S., FARC focused its attention on Europe's swelling four million cocaine consumer market. Taking advantage of the structural weaknesses and widespread corruption of West African governments, FARC *"bribed"* its way into the highest echelons of the ruling political and military elite of countries like Mali, Sierra Leone, Mauritania, Liberia and Guinea-Bissau – involving them in its criminal venture.

The US Drug Enforcement Agency (DEA) recorded several meetings between members of the Al-Qaeda in the Islamic Maghreb and Colombian FARC representatives.

In what some call *"Air Cocaine"*, the drug is continually airlifted from Colombia and Venezuela to numerous landing strips in the Sahel and/or shipped to the coasts Morocco, Algeria and Libya to be on-forwarded to Europe through the Mediterranean. Dispatching and smuggling the drug into Europe is the duty of Islamic extremist groups such as Al-Qaeda and Hezbollah who reap a generous slice of the profits to finance their own terror operations worldwide. So-called *narco-jihadists* are in charge of protecting and shipping the drug mainly through Spain, Italy and Turkey into the European continent.

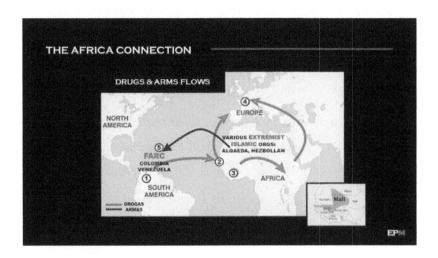

"After arriving by boat or by air from Latin America, the largest share of the cocaine quickly leaves West Africa on its way to Europe."

Georges Berghezan (GRIP, Groupe de Recherche et d'Information sur la Paix et la Sécurité)

Drug smuggling is certainly not new to Africa. FARC and other Latin American drug cartels have been connected to the powerful Nigerian Mafia for many years *(and recently with Boko Haram)*. However, with northern Africa now transformed into one of the world's busiest drug trafficking spots, cocaine traffic has definitely established as one of Africa's most important illegal activities.

The metaphoric intent of the common expression *"tip of the iceberg"* can hardly be better served than in the case of TOC. When a drug shipment is intercepted, dozens more are making it to their destination. When a weapons cache is discovered, it is certainly part of a much larger and formidable arsenal. When a truck stuffed with illegal immigrants is stopped, hundreds more evade the surveillance of border authorities. Similarly, when information on strategic alliances between Islamic extremist terrorist groups and drug trafficking organizations such as FARC comes to light, more ominous intentions are unquestionably behind. The intrinsic underground nature of TOC makes it impossible for anyone to know its real magnitude and even less to detect its next moves. On the other hand, misjudging its threat may turn to be fatal.

"The reach of Latin American illicit trafficking networks
Extends well beyond the region"

Former U.S. diplomat Celina Realuyo

CHAPTER 2

THE MASTER PLAN

I.   OBJECTIVE

To challenge U.S. authority in Latin America by establishing significant presence in the region, building meaningful alliances with like-minded governments, setting up conventional and nuclear infrastructure and acquiring operational capability, with the aim of either deterring or attacking the United States of America.

II.   MAIN COHORTS

Islamic Republic of Iran, Cuban Republic, Foro de Sao Paulo, ALBA[7] *"Socialist"* Countries, FARC and Middle East Islamic Terrorist Organizations.

III.   ANCILLARY COHORTS

Transnational Organized Crime Networks, e.g. Mexican and Venezuelan Drug Cartels, FARC collaborators and criminal gangs.

---

[7] ALBA: Alianza Bolivariana para los Pueblos de Nuestra América / Bolivarian Alliance for the Peoples of Our America

IV. KEY SUCCESS FACTORS

- Convergence of Intent
- Stealth & Perseverance
- Loyalty, Permanence & Persistence
- Strategic Asymmetric Warfare

EL PLAN MAESTRO (THE MASTER PLAN)
ISLAMIC EXTREMISM IN LATIN AMERICA

V. CONVERGENCE OF INTENT

Not everything went as planned in the attacks perpetrated by Al Qaeda against the Twin Towers and the Pentagon on September 11, 2001. Had *United Airlines Flight 93* culminated its mission, the White House would have also been in flames. But even this would have been largely insufficient for perpetual U.S. enemies such as the Islamic Republic of Iran and other Islamic extremist groups. For these, regardless of their Islamic affiliation[8], the 9/11 attacks represented

---

[8] The 9/11 attacks were perpetrated by Al Qaeda, a terrorist group which adheres to Islam's Sunni sect. The Islamic Republic of Iran is affiliated to Islam's Shia sect.

merely a scratch to the *"evil empire."* And indeed, despite the powerful and wounding message sent to the West in terms of its vulnerability, the U.S. promptly recovered, at least in terms of the physical damage that had been inflicted over the country.

When dealing with Iran, it is always useful to remember its grand hegemonic past under the Great Persian Empire. Unlike the brief history of the Americas, Iran's history dates back more than 5000 years. Five millennia during which the Persian people acquired invaluable wisdom, sturdy resilience and, above all, limitless patience in order to attain their objectives. Iran's Ayatollahs, on the other hand, have unfailingly obeyed the Islamic creed for over 1350 years, ever since Islam became the commanding religion of ancient Persia. Put in other words, while many things have changed since ancient times, nothing will ever change the axiomatic objectives of Islam. These, as we know, involve the subjugation and annihilation of the *"infidels"*, the sworn enemies of Islam.

Hence, the 9/11 attacks, were unfinished business. However, it did not take long for Iran to draw a new plan that would achieve higher impact and more definitive results, and this plan has already been underway in the US *backyard* for several years. During the last decade, Iran has stealthily and patiently forged sinister alliances with *"socialist"* governments that share their hostility against the U.S. and with criminal organizations, such as Colombia's FARC, which obey their own mandatory creed.

VI.   STEALTH & PERSEVERANCE

Patience and perseverance are two of Islam's fundamental precepts, and these gain further relevance when their purpose is to wage the *Jihad* or *Holy War*. Patience is a condition for success and prosperity which doubles the rewards for those who practice it. Several Quranic verses refer to the value of applying the instruments of patience and perseverance in order to be successful in this and in the other world.

The cautiousness, patience and perseverance involved in the execution of the 9/11 attacks is a perfect example. Planning and preparation for the despicable acts of terror started several years before, providing the required time for proper execution. During this time the material perpetrators learned how to fly in U.S. flight schools and studied every imaginable detail concerning the operation. Targets well carefully selected in advance and operational implications judiciously analyzed. Access routes to airports, air routes and flight schedules were assessed, and contingency plans drawn.

It is this same patience and perseverance that Iran and its cohorts have exercised for more than decade in order to implement the strategies of *The Master Plan*. Since 2005, they have been steadily laying the rudimentary foundations for its execution by enabling the penetration of Iran and Islamic terror groups into the region, facilitating the emergence of *"narcopopulist"* governments and allowing for the expansion of narcoterrorist organizations such as Colombia's FARC.

VII. LOYALTY, PERMANENCE AND PERSISTENCE

Referring to the term *loyalty* when discussing politics may seem like a contradiction in terms. Nonetheless, *The Master Plan*'s success largely depends on the *loyalty* and unconditional adherence to its long term objectives by each of its cohorts. While the duration of this allegiance may vary in function of the achievement of mutual and/or individual objectives, the fundamental bond between them will most certainly remain unchanged, i.e. their shared animosity towards the United States of America.

Another of *The Master Plan*'s essential ingredients is the maintenance of the political *status quo* and the permanence in power of governments which are involved in the plot. The risk of a substantive political change in any of these countries could translate into a major hurdle and could entail significant adjustments. Permanence in power, at any cost, is hence indispensable in order to ensure the unobstructed continuity of the plan. To date, the majority of *"socialist"* Latin American leaders involved in the plan have managed to be successively re-elected, namely, Venezuela's Nicolás Maduro, Colombia's Juan Manuel Santos, Brazil's Dilma Roussef, Ecuador's Rafael Correa, Bolivia's Evo Morales and Nicaragua's Daniel Ortega[9]. Then again, the integrity of each and every one of the respective electoral processes has been vigorously contested by opposition parties, based on credible allegations of widespread vote rigging and electoral fraud.

---

[9] Although Argentina's former President Cristina Fernández de Kirchner was also reelected, she lost the November 2015 race in which Mauricio Macri, a center-right opposition candidate, was elected.

The inherent unpredictability of geopolitical developments requires unwavering persistence in the event of an unanticipated significant occurrence. The advent of such an occurrence must not distract or deviate cohorts from working towards the overarching objectives of *The Master Plan*.

Seen in retrospect, this precautionary measure has proven its relevance. Major and significant changes, such as the Arab Spring and the death of Hugo Chávez have transpired since the plan's inception, nonetheless, its overall implementation remains practically unscathed. Iran continues to strengthen and expand its presence in the region, *Bolivarian* governments remain in power and FARC has perceptibly augmented and expanded its criminal enterprise.

VIII. STRATEGIC ASYMMETRIC WARFARE

While *The Master Plan*'s intrinsic covert nature allows only for an educated guess to be made in relation to its operational strategy, the *"asymmetric warfare"* concept which addresses substantial differences between the forces of two or more opponents, has recurrently emerged. This theory was developed in China in 496 B.C. by *Sun Tzu*, one of the most outstanding military strategists of all times. *Sun Tzu*'s "military strategy" theory stated that *"asymmetric warfare"* inevitably entailed the use of tactics such as "deception" and "surprise" in order to level forces with the stronger opponent.

IX. ORGANIZATIONAL & SUPPORT STRUCTURES

One way to visualize *The Master Plan* is to portray it in a pattern of concentric circles, where the main cohorts are positioned in the inner-most circle and ancillary cohorts occupy the outer circles, in function of their role. The inner circle comprises Iran, Cuba, Venezuela, Colombia's FARC and Hezbollah. These are responsible for one or more duties compatible with their respective field of expertise and capabilities.

Political lobbying is mainly the responsibility of governments, but it may also include other actors such as the Foro de Sao Paulo, UNASUR or FARC. Technical assistance and logistics support are provided by FARC, Hezbollah and Mexican Cartels, or by any member of the TOC network. A good example of the type of support that can be made available by TOC groups is the provision of safe passage to Islamic terrorists via tunnels used for drugs, arms and people smuggling, located on the US's southern border. These groups are also able to provide weapons, snipers, false documents and other pertinent supplies.

Amongst the alternatives for the location of nuclear sites are primarily Cuba, Colombia and Venezuela, in view of the convenience of their strategic location *vis-à-vis* the U.S.'s southern coast. An additional option is placing the missile launch base on a vessel in the territorial waters of countries like Nicaragua, or in those of affiliated small-island countries in the Caribbean Sea.

If, like in October 1962, the U.S. President announces that nuclear-tipped missiles are pointing towards the U.S. from its *backyard*, *The Master Plan* will have achieved its deleterious objective.

THE CUBAN MISSILE CRISIS

On October 14, 1962, a U-2 spy plane flying over Cuba discovered nuclear missile sites under construction. These missiles would have been capable of reaching the United States. President Kennedy convened a small group of senior officials to debate the crisis which met almost uninterruptedly during the next two weeks. The group was split between those who wanted a military solution, such as an invasion or air strikes, and those who sought a diplomatic solution to put an end to the crisis.

Eight days later, President John F. Kennedy ordered a naval blockade of Cuba while U.S. military forces prepared ICBMs for launch, dispatched Polaris submarines and B-52 bombers which were placed on maximum alert. As the world watched events unfold, tensions between the U.S. and the Soviet Union augmented. Reconnaissance flights continued over Cuba and U.S. and Soviet officials exchanged words of warning.

Following extensive negotiations, on October 28, Soviet Union Premier Nikita Khrushchev announced the withdrawal of the missiles from Cuban territory. The Cuban missile crisis is deemed to be the closest the world has ever come to a catastrophic nuclear dispute. According to information that emerged years later, the missiles the Soviet Union had positioned in Cuba were operational and were armed with functional nuclear warheads.

CHAPTER 3

RADICAL ISLAM THRIVES IN THE US "BACKYARD"

Backyards require care. Negligence may lead to the excessive growth of weed where rodents can hide, or even worse, your annoying neighbor may decide to plant his own seeds and bear the fruits of the harvest. Knowing him, he may even claim its property in view of your total neglect.

Before the seventh Summit of the Americas in Panama City, U.S. President Barack Obama told Latin American leaders that the days when his country freely interfered in regional affairs were over. *"Days of meddling in Latin America are past"*, he said. What President Obama manifestly hasn't figured out is that if the U.S. doesn't *"meddle"* in its own *backyard*, others will, and those who already have are not precisely the U.S.'s best friends.

While neglect for Latin America in terms of U.S. foreign policy dates back to beginning of the 90's, under Barack Obama things got tangibly worse, both for the countries in the region as for the U.S. itself. As we will see in further detail in Chap 7, under Obama's watch *anti-US "narcopopulist"* governments multiplied, the Islamic Republic of Iran extended its influence and forged somber connections across the region, radical Islam grew immoderately and, as mentioned in the previous chapter, TOC had the chance to thrive.

In sum, America has practically lost its *backyard*. Tangled in domestic challenges and the Middle East and Asia, it has grossly underestimated the strategic importance of Latin America, allowing others to take the lead. Ironically, most of those who have taken that lead are the same foes the U.S. is struggling to defeat abroad. Moreover, Russia and China have also taken advantage of U.S. absence and have vigorously extended their strategic, military and economic influence throughout the region.

I.   IRAN & LATIN AMERICA

Iran's presence in Latin America dates back to the days of Khomeini's Islamic revolution in 1979, when Cuba's Fidel Castro recognized the Ayatollah Khomeini as the leader of the new *Islamic Republic of Iran,* helping to legitimize the *Islamic Revolution* that overthrew Shah Reza Pahlavi. The animosity of the Castro regime and that of the Islamic leaders against the U.S. contributed to the forging of solid political ties between the two countries which still remain strong today. However, Iran's penetration into Latin America during Cold War times met many obstacles, the main one being the

THE SHOW IS ON: THE IRANIAN THREAT

In December 2011, Mexico's *UNIVISION* TV channel presented *"The Iranian Threat"*, a documentary film about a plan designed to launch a massive attack on US government computer systems which also included the possibility of conducting a physical offensive. Recordings and testimonies gathered by *UNIVISION* reveal how Mexico City-based diplomats from Iran, Venezuela and Cuba had promoted and financed the scheme, aimed at blocking and eventually destroying the servers of the White House, the FBI, the Pentagon, and those of the US's main nuclear facilities. According to witnesses, the original idea of the attack had originated in the Cuban embassy and it had later been endorsed by the diplomatic missions of the Islamic Republic of Iran and Venezuela. These same witnesses corroborated that the scheme had also considered the possibility of conducting armed attacks against the US.

Muhammad Hassan Ghadiri, Iran's ambassador to Mexico at the time, flatly denied the accusations despite the fact that incriminating recordings obtained by undercover agents proved otherwise. These same recordings revealed the involvement of Livia Acosta, Venezuela's Consul in Miami and a former cultural attaché to the Venezuelan Embassy in Mexico. Acosta was tasked with obtaining information on access codes to servers of US nuclear plants, in order for it to be personally conveyed to President Hugo Chávez. Following the uncovering of the plot in 2012, Acosta was declared *persona non grata* and was subsequently expelled from the US.

U.S.'s close vigilance over its *backyard.* The Islamic nation would have to wait until the war was over for things to begin to change.

I.1   AND THINGS CHANGED

Shortly after the election of Iranian President Mahmoud Ahmadinejad in 2005, Iran declared Latin America a foreign policy priority. Since then, Iran has been tirelessly working to expand its influence in the region. Ahmadinejad paid several a visits to the region in which he visited Venezuela, Ecuador, Cuba and Nicaragua. As previously mentioned, Iran had found in the new *"narcopopulist"* governments the ideal allies to further its *anti-US* agenda in the region. The Iranian president traveled to Cuba several times during his tenure and was amiably received by the decade's old Latin American dictatorship. In Ahmadinejad's own words: *"Our positions are very similar, the two countries share the same antagonism against the Americans and will continue to fight together. We have been good friends, we still are and we will always be. Long live Cuba!"*

Under Ahmadinejad, Iran's investment in Cuba tripled and numerous commercial agreements involving tariff reductions in products ranging from industrial machinery to textiles were signed. The fact that both countries were subject to trade sanctions by the U.S. further solidified their relationship and resulted in mutual support in terms of their evasion.

Iran owes its expansion in Latin America to Venezuela's Hugo Chávez. Chávez considered its relations with Iran *"a sacred matter"* and literally laid a red carpet for the Islamic republic to penetrate the region. He personally interceded with governments of the region on behalf of Iran, oftentimes backing his good offices with oil or with attractive sums of money. In coordination with Ecuador and other countries in the region, Chávez set up a complex financial network to help Iran circumvent international sanctions imposed by the U.S. and Europe, which restricted Iran from making use of the international banking system. Before Ahmadinejad's arrival to power Iranian investment in Latin America was merely symbolic. Following the rapprochement between the two nations the figure reached over US $ 40 billion, only in regards to Venezuela. According to journalist Manuchehr Honarmand, an Iranian dissident who was imprisoned in Venezuela for three years, Iranian government agents are now involved in all the sectors of the Venezuelan economy.

In recent years Iran increased the number of embassies in Latin America from six to eleven and placed members of the notorious members of its Quds force *(the Elite Force of the Iranian Revolutionary Guards)*, in various diplomatic posts throughout the region. Embassies such as the one in Caracas, Venezuela and Managua, Nicaragua are staffed with hundreds of Iranian diplomats.

I.2   MILITARY EXPANSION

Since 2005, Iran has established an unprecedented military and intelligence presence all over Latin America. A strategic alliance between Venezuela and Iran and close military cooperation between the two countries has allowed the Islamic nation to increase its strategic capabilities in the Western Hemisphere. Multiple agreements have been signed with Venezuela and other *Bolivarian* nations such as Ecuador and Bolivia for the supply of defense, intelligence, security and energy assistance by Iran. Through these military alliances Iran has already taken bold steps in order to establish

THE PARAGUANÁ MISSILE BASE

In May 2011 the German newspaper Die Weld confirmed that Iran and Venezuela had signed an agreement for the installation of a missile manufacturing base in Venezuela's Paraguaná peninsula, some 75 miles away from the Colombian border. According to Die Weld, a group of engineers belonging to Iran's Revolutionary Guard had traveled covertly to Venezuela in order to implement the project, their main task being to focus on facilitating the possibility of launching airstrikes capable of reaching other countries in the region, including the U.S. This involved the construction of command stations, residential areas, security towers and bunkers, as well as the acquisition of warheads, rocket fuel and other items required for the construction of the missile base.

its conventional and nuclear military capabilities in the region, including the creation of Quds Forces command and control centers in Bolivia and Venezuela. Today, even the Venezuelan president's bodyguards receive training and counseling from Iranian and Cuban advisers.

I.3   A RENEWED FRIENDSHIP

Despite abrupt changes since the times of Hugo Chávez and Mahmoud Ahmadinejad, bilateral relations between the two countries have remained practically intact. Nonetheless, while mutual high-level visits in the past pursued broad strategic cooperation, President Nicolás Maduro's visits to the Islamic nation have dealt more with the price of oil and/or with Venezuela requesting loans from Iran, in view of the country's economic collapse.

Many analysts were attentive to the impact the death of Hugo Chávez would have over the relationship between Venezuela and Iran. In an effort to maintain the ship afloat, Iran's Ahmadinejad traveled to Venezuela to attend Chávez's funeral services and reiterated Iran's commitment to support Venezuela's *"Bolivarian* Revolution."* The Iranian president went to the extent of calling Hugo Chávez a *prophet,* comparing him both to a prominent Shia Imam and to Jesus Christ. This audacious statement generated a forceful reaction on the part of influential Shia clerics in Iran who cautioned Ahmadinejad to refrain from making such declarations. In any case, all this clamor proved to be futile, as both countries swiftly resumed communication under the government of Venezuela's new President Nicolás Maduro.

In January 2015, the presidents of Iran and Venezuela reiterated their common stance against US *"imperialism"*, and insisted on the need for multilateral cooperation between Tehran and Caracas to expand. President Rouhani emphasized that *"the development of relations with Latin American countries was among the policies of the 11th government."* He also urged Venezuela to re-establish the Caracas-Tehran air route which, according to Rouhani, would make the Iranian and the Venezuelan nations more acquainted with each other and would encourage further commercial exchanges.

Towards the end of 2015, ayatollah Ali Khamenei himself praised Venezuela's struggle to free itself from U.S. pressure, adding that Iran considered Venezuela's progress and success as his being its own. Both Iran's Supreme Leader and the Venezuelan President reiterated their commitment to combat U.S. *"arrogance"* in the world, agreeing that the only way to move forward was through "resistance." The Iranian leader added that the objective of the U.S. was to *"destroy the inspiring resistance of the Venezuelan Government and the Venezuelan people."*

I.4   IRAN'S TERROR NETWORK EXPANDS

Iran has amply expanded its terror network in Latin America. More than 40,000 of the regime's agents have reportedly been placed in the region, mainly in Venezuela, Bolivia, Ecuador, Brazil, Guatemala and Nicaragua. Along with the members of the Quds Forces, Iran's contingent is composed of security, intelligence and propaganda agents, including former interrogators and torturers from Iran and from other countries such as Afghanistan, Lebanon, Iraq and Somalia. Their main mission is to spread the Islamic ideology of the regime, gather military intelligence and prepare for the *global jihad*. In the words of Hassan Rahim Pour Azghodi, a member of Iran's Supreme Council who visited the region, *"it is necessary to cause an international Jihad; we should not fear anyone."*

I.5   BOLIVIA: IRAN'S NEW LEADING ALLY

Another country diligently courted by Iran has been Bolivia, which lies today at the forefront of Iran's relentless effort to expand its presence and influence in the US *backyard*. In 2007, Iran's Ahmadinejad paid the first visit ever by an Iranian Head of State to the South American country, and found in Bolivia's Evo Morales fertile grounds to implement his agenda. Morales, perhaps one of the most vocal of Latin American leaders in terms of his *anti-US* stance, said that the establishment of bilateral relations with Iran *"was a sign of the determination to fight together against the US and its interference in Latin American and Middle Eastern affairs."*

Iran military cooperation with Bolivia is one of the most robust in the history of the Latin American country. It ranges from the acquisition of aircraft and helicopter gunships, to the launch of an atomic program. During one of President Evo Morales' visits to Iran, a deal was signed in which Bolivia would buy Iranian-made aircraft and helicopters in order for these to be used in the training of the Bolivian Air Force. The deal included a team of Iranian technicians in charge of providing maintenance to the military aircraft.

President Evo Morales met with Iranian President Hassan Rouhani and the country's supreme leader Ali Khamenei in a visit to Teheran in November 2015. Both countries validated their concurrence in the realm of international affairs and vowed to boost cooperation and bilateral ties. In Morales' words *"Bolivia and Iran are countries that share similar interests in their struggle against imperialism."* Morales has also received Iran's backing in the context of Bolivia's dispute with its neighbor Chile to have access to the sea (Bolivia lost 400 km of coastline and 120,000 km^2 of territory as a result of a military confrontation with Chile in 1879).

I.6   A JOB WELL DONE

One of Iran's main political achievements within the context of its political *rapprochement* to Latin America was the support it managed to gather from most of the region's governments in order to gain access to nuclear energy. Cuba's Castro, Brazil's Lula da Silva and Venezuela's Hugo Chávez offered Iran unconditional support to its nuclear aspirations and fervently defended the country's right to have access to "peaceful" nuclear technology. The majority of Latin American governments vigorously endorsed Iran's claims at the UN and other international fora, including the International Atomic Energy Agency (IAEA). Ecuador's President Rafael Correa played the leading role in the issuance of a joint declaration by the ALBA countries in support to the Government of Iran and its nuclear program. This initiative is largely attributed to the fact that, after Venezuela and Bolivia, Ecuador has been the country that has interacted the most with Iran in the region, both in the realm of military cooperation and in the context of Iran's intense search for uranium across the subcontinent.

THE "ALBA" SCHOOL OF DEFENSE

The special guest at the opening ceremony of the *School of Defense of the Bolivarian Alternative for the Americas (ALBA)* was Iran's Defense Minister Ahmad Vahid, one of the alleged perpetrators of the 1994 Buenos Aires terrorist attacks on a Jewish cultural center. Part of the funding for the establishment of this new institution which opened in June 2011 in the town of Warnes in Bolivia had been made available by Iran, together with some 300 instructors and technicians from the Iranian Revolutionary Guard.

The school's purported mission was to set up a *rapid intervention force* composed of *Bolivarian* Militia from various countries in the region. Upon inaugurating the premises, Bolivia's President Evo Morales thanked Iran for its invaluable contribution to the *Bolivarian* revolution, and insisted on the need to get rid of US intelligence agencies in Latin America *"in order to win the asymmetric battle against imperialism."* Morales also requested that the UN Security Council be abolished.

GHOST FLIGHTS

In 2007, a secret and frequent pilgrimage between Venezuela and Iran raised the suspicion of US authorities. Since March that year an *Iran Air* Boeing 747 had begun to shuttle between Tehran and Caracas - via Damascus, Syria. Only a few months later, *Conviasa*, Venezuela's main airline, had followed the same steps as its counterpart and had opened regular flights through the same route.

The flight manifests of the enigmatic *"ghost flights"* (dubbed as such by employees of Caracas's Simon Bolívar airport), dodged any kind of "official" customs control, and both the cargo and the passengers were exempted from undergoing any kind of immigration procedures. These suspicions were later confirmed by Italian newspaper *La Stampa* which reported that several *Conviasa* flights had been transporting intelligence officials, military officers and illicit materials from Iran to Venezuela, including components for a ballistic missile program, and weapons for Colombia's FARC.

I.7 THE ARGENTINA DOSSIER

Dr. Alberto Nisman - an Argentine special prosecutor in charge of the investigation of the 1994 bombing of a Jewish community center in Buenos Aires - was found shot in his home on January 18, 2015, a few hours before he was to present his most recent findings before the Argentine congress. According to the Argentinian government, Nisman had committed suicide, a version that many Argentinians did not take for granted. Nisman was about to open a Pandora box which would reveal obscure dealings between Argentina's President Cristina Fernández de Kirchner's and the Government of Iran.

OBAMA SIGNS LAW COUNTERING IRANIAN SWAY IN LATIN AMERICA

The 28th of December, 2012, U.S. President Barack Obama enacted a law targeting Iran's alleged influence in Latin America. The act also calls on the Department of Homeland Security to bolster surveillance at U.S. borders with Canada and Mexico to "prevent operatives from Iran, the Iranian Revolutionary Guard Corps, and its Quds Force, Hezbollah or any other terrorist organization from entering the United States."

Iran's relationship with Argentina has been one filled with secrecy, controversy, ambiguity and death. During the nineties Argentina was the victim of Middle Eastern style terrorism. In 1992 a bomb destroyed the Israeli Embassy in Buenos Aires and two years later, in 1994, the above mentioned attack on the Jewish community center (AMIA[10]) killed eighty-five people and left more than three hundred wounded. Both acts of terrorism were attributed to *Hezbollah* which had reportedly acted under the orders of the Government of Iran. The investigation led by Argentinian authorities and Interpol stated that nine Iranian citizens had been involved in the terrorist acts and that among these were former Iranian president Ali Rafsanjani and Iranian Defense Minister Ahmad Vahidi. The Government of Iran categorically denied any involvement in the attacks.

While the reestablishment of relations between the two countries depended to a large extent on the resolution of the issue of the Buenos Aires terrorist attacks

---

[10] AMIA - Asociación Mutual Israelita Argentina

and, despite lasting resentment on the part of many Argentinians *vis-a-vis* Iran due to its alleged participation, the appearance of Venezuela's Hugo Chávez on the stage triggered a radical change in the Argentinian Government's posture towards the issue.

As Iran's main representative in the region and aware of Iran's interest to establish nuclear ties with Argentina, Chávez played the role of mediator between the two governments, which included generous financial favors to Argentina's President Kirchner who was striving to cope with the country's serious economic crisis. At the request of Hugo Chávez, Kirchner took the political decision to approach the Iranians. After intense political lobbying, the Argentine parliament approved an agreement with Iran which generated enormous controversy and which was widely criticized both inside and outside the country. The Jewish community, in particular, feared that the attacks of the previous decade would sink into oblivion and that impunity would prevail, despite the fact that their authorship had always been clear.

What Alberto Nisman had been claiming from the onset was that Iran had been actively setting up intelligence and operational structures in Latin America, and that it had been establishing terrorist networks throughout the region for decades. Nisman said that Iran's intelligence activities in Latin America were being conducted either by Iranian officials or by the Islamic militant group Hezbollah. He added that "Criminal plans" by Iran could be under way in Brazil, Colombia, Chile, Paraguay, Uruguay, Suriname, and Trinidad and Tobago.

The latest chapter of this saga involved Antonio Stiuso – former Head of the Secretariat of State Intelligence Operations Department. On March 1st 2016, Stiuso declared before a judge that the former prosecutor of the AMIA case Alberto Nisman *"had been killed by a group linked to the government, as a result of his accusations against former President Cristina Kirchner."* He added that the perpetrators of the crime had wanted to make it look like a suicide. Stiuso did not hesitate to point his finger to whom he believed was responsible for the unfortunate events that had been transpiring: *"The author of all this madness, was that woman, Cristina Fernández de Kirchner"*, he said.

"For their part, since October 2011, policymakers in Washington have begun to pay serious attention to Tehran's activities in the Western Hemisphere. Yet they have done little concrete to respond to it, at least so far. Unless and until such a strategy does emerge, Tehran's Latin American efforts—and the threats posed by them to American interests and the U.S. homeland—will only continue to expand."

Ilan Berman - American Foreign Policy Council

II.   MIDDLE EASTERN IMMIGRATION INTO LATIN AMERICA

Latin America has been the subject of several immigration waves from the Middle East and Southeast Asia throughout its history. The first migrations took place during the colonial period, when Syrian and Lebanese communities, both of Muslim and Christian origin, traveled across the Atlantic and settled in various countries in the region and, in particular, in the Caribbean Sea. Over time, these communities integrated with native ones and after a few generations, most of them converted to Christianity. During the second half of the 20th century new migratory movements occurred after World War II and the Cold War. Muslims who were part of more recent migrations tended to be more orthodox and devout to Islam than the previous ones. Today, Latin America counts some 6 million adherents to Islam amongst which 1.5 million live in Brazil and 700,000 in Argentina, the two countries that host the two largest Muslim minorities in South America.

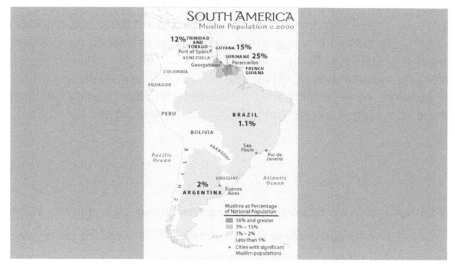

Source: Islam Project

Large Muslim communities can also be found in Guyana, Suriname, and Trinidad and Tobago. U.S. government security sources reported that a number of extremist Islamic organizations had called their attention in Trinidad and Tobago, a country with more than a million Muslims. Among these, the more notorious one is *Jamaat al Muslimeen*, a Muslim organization composed of Sunni and Shia Muslim immigrants from the Middle East and South Asia.

II.1   ISLAMIC PROSELYTISM

There are clear indications of the growing power and spread of the Islamist ideology in Latin America and both Iran and Hezbollah have played a key role. Spreading the Islamic faith and promoting the *Jihad* or *Holy War* has been at the forefront of their agenda. Groups composed of Shia missionaries whose core mission is to convert the most vulnerable communities to Islam have been deployed throughout the region. These target mainly poor indigenous groups which, due to their dismal living conditions are more susceptible to conversion, such as the Wayuu tribe in Colombia and Venezuela (see box), and Maya Indians in Chiapas, a depressed zone in southern Mexico.

A growing number of native people has now converted to Islam and amongst these several cases of extreme conversion and radicalization of individuals have been seen. The most promising amongst these are sent to the holy city of Qom in Iran, to be trained in anti-guerrilla warfare and to deepen the practice of Islam. According to the German publication *Der Spiegel*, new followers recruited among the indigenous Mayans in southern Mexico are reportedly converting by the hundreds. More recently, the U.S. Southern Command said that about 100 people from countries in the Caribbean and South America had joined ISIS.

"Iran has established 80-plus "cultural centers" across Latin America and the Caribbean to promote Shiite Islam, counter U.S. influence in the region, and increase its own."

Southcom Commander Gen. John Kelly in 2015 before the US Congress

THE WAYUU TRIBE

One of the most revealing examples of progress made by Iran and Hezbollah in the context of their Islamic proselytizing campaign in Latin America is that of the indigenous Wayuu tribe which inhabits both sides of the Colombia-Venezuela border - in the Guajira Peninsula. The Wayuu were one of the few tribes who managed to survive the Spanish conquest and thus preserved its ancestral customs almost intact.

Photo: Web

Today, many Wayuu women and girls are wearing the Islamic veil, as children and young men and women learn the Koran as a substitute for any other type of education. Tuition includes religious indoctrination and military training. Recruits are trained in the use of all kinds of weapons and explosives.

Future *suicide bombers* are selected among the youngest and amongst those who have become more radical in terms of honoring Islam's sacred objectives. Both men and women are submitted to individual initiation regimes in order to be converted into human bombs. Training and indoctrination are based on the concept of *suicidal terrorism with religious consent*, a concept overtly promoted by the Iranian regime in the modern Middle East. According to this view, when suicide involves the removal or extermination of the enemy of Islam, it is glorified, blessed and rewarded by Allah.

III.   LATIN AMERICA: A "TERRORIST NEST"

It is widely admitted that the presence Islamic extremist terrorist groups in Latin America has been steadily increasing. Counterterrorism experts claim that cells linked to Hezbollah, Jihad and Al Qaeda are well established in the region and operate in countries like Argentina, Ecuador, Honduras, Mexico, Nicaragua, Paraguay, Uruguay and Colombia.

Hezbollah, the *Party of Allah* and Iran's armed terrorist branch, is at the forefront of this initiative. Its presence in Latin America was revitalized by Hugo Chávez who paved the way for the terrorist group to expand its presence the region. Hezbollah publicly declared its sympathy for Hugo Chávez and the *"Bolivarian Revolution"*, and endorsed its *anti-Zionist* and *anti-imperialist* position. Chávez, in turn, offered shelter to Hezbollah and other Islamic terrorists groups such as Islamic Jihad and Al Qaeda, and issued passports and visas to thousands of people in the Middle East, including instructors, operators, recruiters and Hezbollah activists.

Hezbollah currently maintains a regional base in Venezuela from which it coordinates its operational cells throughout the region. It is in charge of promoting Islamic values and distributing Islamic propaganda across the continent and reports on the activities of subsidiary cells in countries like Mexico, Argentina, Colombia, El Salvador and Chile.

Latin America constitutes one of Hezbollah's main operational and fundraising bases. In December 2011, the *New York Times* revealed the extensive and complex links between Hezbollah and cocaine trafficking in South America. High level Hezbollah officials are directly involved in cocaine trafficking in partnership with the region's most violent drug cartels such as Colombia's FARC and Mexico's Zetas. The terrorist group is also involved in arms and human trafficking, and donations from thousands of supporters in the region, mostly of Arab origin, also contribute to the group's finances.

"They (Hezbollah) - are more involved in the cocaine trade than ever before, and have greater access in the region due their allies in Venezuela, Ecuador, Bolivia and elsewhere...they have more freedom of movement and fewer restrictions. This has greatly increased their capacity to carry out intelligence operations, train and position operatives and prepare attacks, particularly if Israel or the U.S. strikes Iran's nuclear facilities."

Douglas Farah, International Assessment and Strategy Center

OPERATION TITAN

In 2008, during what Colombian authorities called *"Operation Titan"* a criminal organization dedicated to drug trafficking linked to **HEZBOLLAH** was dismantled.

The organization's reach reportedly extended to the US, Europe, the Middle East, Africa, Asia and Central America. The operation resulted in more than 100 people in several countries being arrested and in the seizure of drugs, aircraft, jewelry and cash.

III.1 HEZBOLLAH IN MEXICO

The district of Chiapas in southern Mexico is famous for the confrontation between the Zapatista National Liberation Front and the Government of Mexico in 1994. Chiapas, which has become a battleground of the war on drugs is also the nerve center of radical Islamist activity in the country. The *Center for Investigation and National Security of Mexico (CISEN)*, had previously alerted the Mexican government about possible support being provided by the Iranian

Embassy in Mexico to the *Mexican Movement of Solidarity with the Iranian People*, presumed to be composed of individuals close to Hezbollah.

In March 2009, the *Washington Times* reported that pro-Iranian group Hezbollah was exploiting cross-border routes between Mexico and the U.S. for drugs and human trafficking, in partnership with the powerful and feared Mexican drug cartels. Furthermore, the Intelligence Committee of the U.S. House of Representatives reported in recent years that links between Mexican cartels with Iran and Hezbollah were being strengthened, and reiterated that Hezbollah was fully involved in drug and weapons trafficking to and from Mexico.

III.2   THE TRIPLE FRONTIER

The **Triple Frontera** or Tri-Border area, where Brazil, Argentina and Paraguay intersect, has long been amongst the most dangerous borders in Latin America. The area is known for the presence of dangerous organized crime groups from all over the world which take advantage of the reigning lawlessness in the neighborhood. These are mainly involved in drug trafficking, human trafficking, prostitution, smuggling and terrorism. Experts estimate that the volume of money that circulates in the area to be in the range of US $ 2 to 3 trillion, annually.

Authorities of the three countries are aware of the fact that Hezbollah, Al Qaeda and Hamas are there, among other extremist groups that have sought refuge in the area. The presence of Islamic terrorist organizations in the Tri-Border zone is largely attributed to the large number of Arab expatriates that inhabit the area, currently estimated at about 25,000 people. Graffiti in Arabic calling for Islamic *Jihad* has been seen in the streets of the three countries.

III.3   AL QAEDA & OTHER INTRUDERS

Experts claim that Al Qaeda has already intruded in several Latin American countries. In April 2011, the Brazilian magazine *VEJA* reported that at least twenty people affiliated with Al Qaeda, Hezbollah and Hamas were taking refuge in Brazil. Pentagon officials also confirmed that human smuggling rings in Latin America had been attempting to sneak Al-Qaeda operatives into the U.S. using false identities. *"People with Middle Eastern names have adopted Hispanic last names before coming into the US."* It has reportedly also been increasingly common for Muslims from Mexico to change their Islamic surnames to Hispanic-sounding names to make moving across the border easier.

But Hezbollah and Al Qaeda are not alone. There is also information about the presence of the Islamic Jihad, Hamas and other Islamic extremist groups in several Caribbean islands, as well as dozens of independent groups inspired by religious edicts or *fatwas* issued by religious leaders in the Middle East. In June 2007, US authorities announced they had disarmed a plot by four Afro-Caribbean converts to Islam from Guyana, and Trinidad and Tobago. The plot pretended to cause maximum chaos and destruction by triggering the explosion of fuel tanks at the John F. Kennedy International Airport in New York, aiming at setting airport facilities and other aircraft on fire.

"Hezbollah represents a significant potential threat to the United States."

Ilan Berman - American Foreign Policy Council

IV. THE "IRAN DEAL" & LATIN AMERICA

London's British Museum exhibits a ceramic cylinder found in Iraq which contains cuneiform writings and has been the object of admiration of historians, philosophers, politicians and religious figures for centuries. The cylinder's writings describe the conquest of Babylon by Cyrus the Great, King of Persia, some five hundred years before Christ. Aside from victory itself, the fact that Cyrus had led the battle increased the world's appreciation for the unique discovery. At that time, Cyrus proclaimed freedom for religious minorities and became one of the main references of Iran's glorious past under the Great Persian Empire.

Things could not be more different in today's Iran. The Iranian regime denies its citizens basic freedoms such as freedom of speech, freedom of religion and freedom of the press. Women, homosexuals, and religious and ethnic minorities are systematically persecuted, and any sign of political dissent results in brutal repression.

Following the election of Mahmoud Ahmadinejad as President in 2005, the Islamic republic's anti-American and *anti-Zionist* stance intensified. Dress codes and Islamic customs began to resurface, as did violent persecution of ethnic minorities. Ahmadinejad led a racist campaign against the Jewish people, denying the Nazi Holocaust and repeatedly threatening to *wipe Israel off the map*.

In June 2013, Iran elected Hasan Rouhani as its new president. Rouhani represented a moderate reformist profile and the hope for change in Iran's foreign policy, particularly in regards to its contentious nuclear program. Rouhani, at least apparently, delivered.

On the 14th of July 2015, in the city of Vienna, Iran and the P5+1[11] signed *"the deal"*, which according to U.S. President Barack Obama will prevent Iran from obtaining a nuclear weapon. Iran, on its side, maintains that it has the right to develop a nuclear program for peaceful purposes only. In the Joint Comprehensive Plan of Action (JCPOA) - better known as the *Iran Deal* - Iran agreed to provide the International Atomic Energy Agency (IAEA) greater access and information regarding its nuclear program. The UN agency will be able to investigate suspicious sites or to probe allegations of covert facilities related to uranium enrichment anywhere in the Iranian territory. IAEA inspectors will also have access to uranium mines and mills, and to continuous inspection of centrifuge manufacturing and storage facilities.

In exchange for all of the above, economic sanctions imposed by the UN, U.S. and EU on Iran will be lifted, subject to IAEA certification *(International sanctions had literally shattered Iran's economy)*. Reportedly, Iran will gain access to more than US $ 100 billion in overseas frozen assets and it will be able to make use of the global financial system for trade purposes. The Islamic nation will also be allowed to resume the sale of oil on international markets.

As far as Latin America is concerned, the *Iran Deal* gravely worsens its regional political and security situation. Nowhere in the agenda was Iran's intrusion in the region taken into consideration. Were the threats that Iran's nuclear developments and its frenetic quest for uranium in the region downplayed?

---

[11] The P5+1 is composed of the five permanent members of the United Nations Security Council (China, France, Russia, United Kingdom and the United States) plus Germany and the European Union.

Why is the IAEA's mandate restricted to the Iranian national territory? How will it be able to ascertain that uranium is not being enriched elsewhere on the planet? Were Iran's obscure links with *"narcopopulist"* nations such as Venezuela and Bolivia and international terrorist groups such as FARC displayed? Was the possibility of Iran circumventing the deal's provisions, as it did in the past in order to evade sanctions, considered? Was Iran requested to shed some light in regards to its support for Hezbollah's disquieting expansion in Latin America?

From a broader perspective, it must be made clear that the Islamic Republic of Iran's long-term plans are not set by the incumbent in the presidency but by the Supreme Religious Leader Ayatollah Ali Khamenei. Rouhani is a former nuclear negotiator of the Iranian government and a Shiite cleric whose friendship with Ayatollah Ali Khamenei dates from the time of the Islamic revolution in 1979. Aside from the fact that Rouhani has also called Israel *"The Great Satan"*, Iran's political program is based on Shiite theology which is protected by the Islamic cleric as a whole. The Islamic cleric ascertains that any major decision or law is in strict accordance with Islamic law. Moreover, Ayatollah Ali Khamenei repeatedly refers to an offensive doctrine in which it is imperative to avoid restricting Iranian efforts to simple deterrence in order to preserve the integrity of its national territory. Khamenei stands firm behind Iran's hegemonic project. For the Supreme Leader, Iran's mission must consider - first and foremost - its expansion and its quest for regional hegemony. In the words of Major General Yahya Rahim Safavi, former commander of the Revolutionary Guards: *"Iran must be distinguished as a regional superpower in the Middle East."*

Taking all of the above into consideration, there are some rather obvious questions to be asked. Will Iran ever renounce to its supreme religious objectives? Will it abdicate to its hegemonic project and allow other countries such as Saudi Arabia to emerge as regional powers? And if deterrence is not an option, where does Ayatollah Khamenei's offensive doctrine fit into the Iran Deal? Last but definitely not least, it is worth mentioning that Iran has done all but withdrawn its ominous threat to *wipe Israel off the map.*

In sum, what Latin America really fears is that the lifting of sanctions and the billions of dollars that Iran will have at its disposal as a result of the *Iran Deal* will actually contribute to Iran's menacing and sinister expansion in the region. This would ultimately translate into the strengthening of autocratic *"narcopopulist"* nations and would thereby spread the scourge of Transnational Organized Crime even further. In the light of the nature Iran's activities of the region to date, the legitimacy of this fear can hardly be contested.

CHAPTER 4

FILLING THE US VACUUM

Only when it is the doctor who tells us that our behavior is life threatening do we tend to seriously consider the matter. Likewise, if it is the U.S. military itself that says in regards to U.S. involvement in Latin America that there is *"near-total lack of awareness of threats and the readiness to respond"*, the matter should be taken seriously. This candid admission by U.S. military commanders which realize the real dimension of the threat 21st Latin America poses to U.S. National Security is symptomatic of the de-prioritization of the region in the U.S. foreign policy agenda. And as military aid to the region is reduced, many analysts fail to understand the persistence of Barack Obama's government gross misjudgment in regards to the strategic importance of the US *backyard*. These concerns are heightened by ample and unambiguous evidence in the sense that U.S. foreign policy towards Latin America has opened the door for other countries such as Russia, Iran and China to capitalize on the vacuum. Moreover, it does not take a rocket scientist to assemble the pieces of the region's geopolitical puzzle, in order to understand that, while immediate threats to U.S. National Security may be in the Middle East, America's real existential threat simmers down south.

According to *Stockholm International Peace Research Institute* (SIPRI), the volume of international transfers of major conventional weapons was 14% higher in 2011-2015 than in 2006-2010. Although Latin America ranks 3rd (after East Asia and the Middle East) in the ambit of global arm purchases, military spending in the region since the beginning of the century has risen faster than in the rest of the world. From approximately US $ 25 billion spent by the region a decade ago, today's spending has reached about US $ 50's billon. While this unprecedented growth is largely attributed to the intensification and spread of drug trafficking throughout the region and to the corresponding expansion of organized crime structures, some countries have been spending inordinate amounts of money in their military, including shady investments in the domain of atomic energy.

As previously mentioned, drug trafficking and crime cannot be disconnected. According to Mexico's *Citizens Council for Public Security*'s 2016 annual ranking of the world's most violent cities[12], 41 out of the 50 cities in the list are in Latin America. In drug-submerged Central America, countries like Guatemala, Honduras and El Salvador have been obliged to increase arms and security spending in what has become one of the planets most perilous zones. The growing action of the infamous Mexican Cartels and its propagation throughout the whole sub region has led to deep penetration of the drug industry both in the public and the private ambits. In the meantime, terrifying organized crime groups such as the infamous *Maras* or *street gangs* have emerged (see box). The cities of San Pedro Sula, in Honduras and San Salvador, El Salvador's capital rank 2nd and 3rd amongst the world's most violent cities.

THE MARA SALVATRUCHA

The Mara Salvatrucha, or MS13, is perhaps the most notorious street gang in the Western Hemisphere. While it has its origins in the poor, refugee-laden neighborhoods of 1980s Los Angeles, the gang's reach now extends from Central American nations like El Salvador and through Mexico, the United States, and Canada.

They rob, extort and bully their way into neighborhoods and have gradually turned to transnational crimes such as human smuggling and drug trafficking. Their activities have helped make the Northern Triangle – Guatemala, El Salvador, and Honduras -- the most violent place in the world that is not at war. In October 2012, the US Department of the Treasury labeled the group a "transnational criminal organization," the first such designation for a US street gang."

But South America does not lag far behind. In countries like Venezuela, which during the 20th century enjoyed relative tranquility, crime has literally become a systemic constituent of governance. Venezuela is considered one of the world's most dangerous countries and Caracas, its Capital, ranks 1st in the above-mentioned ranking of the most violent cities. According to the United Nations, only Honduras has a worse murder rate than Venezuela.

---

[12] Source: Business Insider, Jan 26, 2016.

The United Nations says there are more guns in circulation in Latin America than in most regions in the world

On the other hand, in spite of the fact that SIPRI's February 2016 report noted a slowing down of Latin America's *arm race*, a series of *Bolivarian* countries such as Venezuela, Bolivia and Ecuador have either sustained or increased military spending, despite an increasingly deteriorating internal economic situation. These same countries have entered into numerous military cooperation agreements with Russia, Iran and China, while growing state support to organized crime structures has resulted in the rise of illegal arms trafficking in the region.

I.   RUSSIA TAKES OVER

Unlike the stealthy and elusive penetration of TOC into Latin America, the Russian Federation's strong comeback into the region has been both forthright and overt. Cuba's Castro and Venezuela's Chávez are not the only ones to remain pathologically anchored to outdated 20th century political paradigms; apparently Putin's Russia is also reviving the ghosts of the Cold War.

During the last decade, and taking advantage of America's inattentiveness *vis-à-vis* its *backyard*, Russia has managed to gain significant strategic military capabilities in the Western Hemisphere, perhaps greater than in Cold War times. As a result of intensive and persistent diplomatic involvement in Latin America, in particular with *Bolivarian "narcopopulist"* governments such as Venezuela, Bolivia and Ecuador, Russia now has access to ports and airspace in strategic places and Russian forces conduct exercises and surveillance missions close to U.S. shores. In the words of Lt. Gen. Kenneth E. Tovo of US Southern Command *"Russia's aim is the same as it was in the Cold War: to "erode" US influence in the region."*

"We have no fear of the US"

Russian Ambassador in La Paz

Setting aside the benefits that derive from the numerous commercial agreements signed by the Russian Federation with Latin American countries, Vladimir Putin had important geopolitical motives which strongly influenced his move towards the region. On the one hand, Putin utterly resented the fact that NATO had practically reached Russia's doorstep through its expansion towards the East since the end of the Cold War. In order to counter the West's bold steps in Europe, Putin decided that Russia should also get as close as possible to US shores by making out of the conquest Latin America and the Caribbean a foreign policy priority. On the other hand, Russia's pivotal presence in the US *backyard* would become part of Russia's ambition to project itself as a new global power, rather than merely a regional one.

In any case, it would have been very difficult for Russia to find a more enabling geopolitical environment than the one 21st century Latin America put at his feet. What had now changed was the object of the strategic affinity with countries in the region. In lieu of the socialist ideological ties that Russia had established in Cold War times, the new bond was the shared goal to counteract the hegemonic effect of U.S. policies in Latin America and around the world. In that context, Russia has been vigorously supporting the positions of countries that have rejected U.S. interference in their domestic affairs.

Vladimir Putin ordered fourteen days of national mourning in Russia after the death of Hugo Chávez

According to the UK based International Institute for Strategic Studies (IISS), in 2010 the U.S. was overtaken by Russia in the sale of arms to Latin America and has since become the leading seller of weapons to the region. The Russian Federation has signed multiple military cooperation agreements with countries such as Venezuela, Peru, Brazil, Mexico, Bolivia, Ecuador, Uruguay and Colombia. Through these agreements, Russia has mainly provided weapons, police and military training and equipment, intelligence technology and training in nuclear technology.

Russia's best client in the region is Venezuela. Two thirds of the country's arms purchases are of Russian origin, mainly as a result of a US $ 5 billion credit line opened by Russia at the times of Hugo Chávez. The two countries agreed to work in the areas of development and safety of nuclear installations, construction of the experimental nuclear reactors and controlled thermonuclear fusion. Project management and technical inputs were to be the responsibility of *Atomstroyexport*, a Russian company which had been involved in the building of the Bushehr nuclear plant in Iran. Upon signing the agreement with Chávez, Vladimir Putin said: *"We will not make an atomic bomb, hence do not bother us like you do with Iran."*

"One of the problems is that where Russia goes, Russian organized crime inevitably follows.

'Security analyst –Douglas Farah –

International Assessment and Strategy Center

The Russian government has sold at some 3,000 surface-to-air missiles to Latin America in recent years. Rostec[13], a firm involved through its subsidiaries in the sale of military hardware to Venezuela, estimated the value of Russia's arms sales at US $ 12 billion. In addition, Venezuela started the production of Kalashnikov rifles and ammunition with the assistance of Russian state-owned *Rosboronexport*.

Nicaragua and Russia signed the largest agreement ever in the field of military cooperation in the Central America. Many experts have highlighted the preponderance that Nicaragua's military would enjoy in Central America if the military cooperation agreement is fully implemented. After thanking Putin, President Daniel Ortega said that Russia was *"illuminating the planet in its struggle for world peace and justice."*

"According to Russian media Russia will send long-range strategic bombers to patrol the Caribbean Sea and the Gulf of Mexico, in an effort to 'monitor foreign powers' military activities and maritime communications."

Linette Lopez, Business Insider - March 27, 2015

---

[13] Rostec is a Russian state corporation in charge of the development, production, promotion and export of hi-tech industrial products for the civil and defense sectors

I.   LATIN AMERICA GOES CHINESE

And as the U.S. takes a long nap, Chinese millenary wisdom entertains Latin America. Much like Russia, China established close relationships with countries of the *Bolivarian* alliance in order to implement its Latin American agenda. However, as opposed to Russia, China has adopted a *"soft-power"[14]* approach, which relies on the ability to shape the preferences of others through attraction rather than duress or intimidation. While China's close relationship with Hugo Chávez greatly enabled its access to the regional arms market and resulted in a significant increase in the flow of Chinese military technology to the region, the Asian giant's efforts have primarily been of economic character. Guided by its relentless pursuit of supply sources across the globe in order to satisfy the growing demand of its huge population, China has mostly focused its efforts on cooperation in the energy sector and in the procurement of raw materials such as coal, copper, natural gas, iron, steel and soybeans.

> *"China's investment in Latin America is not ideological.*
>
> *It is pragmatic and economic"*
>
> Margaret Myers – Inter American Dialogue

Much like it has done in Africa, China has also become one Latin America's main financing sources. China's loans have less strings attached to them than Western cooperation does, and in view of urgent liquidity needs of many countries in the region and limitations to access global capital markets, these loans have been gratefully welcome. According to the Inter-American Dialogue, China has loaned over US $ 119 billion to Latin American nations in the past decade, primarily receiving oil in exchange. The main beneficiary of these loans has been Venezuela which has received US $ 65 billion since 2007, roughly half

---

[14] The term *"soft power"*, was originally conceived by Harvard Professor Joseph S. Nye in 1990 who maintained that the United States had power and influence reserves other than *"hard power"*, or the projection of military force.

of China's overall loan portfolio. An additional 34 % of Chinese loans was granted to Argentina, Brazil and Ecuador.

Information provided by the Economic Commission for Latin America and the Caribbean (ECLAC) in 2015, revealed that China had taken the European Union's second place in the list of countries that invest the most in Latin America. Although the U.S. remains the region's first trade partner, China is in the lead in trade with Brazil, Argentina, Peru and Venezuela[15].

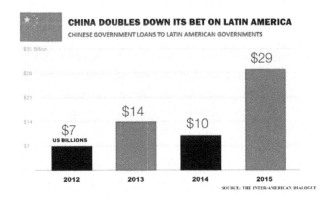

CHINA DOUBLES DOWN ITS BET ON LATIN AMERICA
CHINESE GOVERNMENT LOANS TO LATIN AMERICAN GOVERNMENTS
SOURCE: THE INTER-AMERICAN DIALOGUE

Among China's best friends in Central America is Nicaragua, which as other *Bolivarian* nations holds an unbending *anti-US* stance. Interpreted as an effort to challenge the Panama Canal and to undermine U.S. economic influence in the Caribbean, China has engaged in the construction of a US $ 50 billion, 173-mile canal across Nicaragua. The controversial project has met strong resistance both at the national and international levels, mainly due to its damaging environmental impact.

Contrary to what some analysts have argued, neither China's economic slowdown nor the recession through which countries like Brazil and Venezuela are going through, have affected the Asian giant's investment in Latin America. To put it in perspective, the US $ 29 billion that Chinese state banks loaned to the region in 2015 is larger than the loans granted by the World Bank and the Inter-American Development Bank (IDB), put together. On the other hand, China's investments in Latin America looks far into the future and the Chinese government is well aware of the long term value of the region's oil and mineral

---

[15] M.I.T.

reserves which include gold, coltan, diamonds, lithium, iron ore and bauxite deposits. Furthermore, Chinese President Xi Jinping has pledged to increase trade between his country and Latin America twofold over the next decade to US $ 250 billion.

Last but not least, while China's foreign policy towards the U.S. *backyard* has apparently prioritized economic considerations over geopolitical ones, the latter invariably underpin the former. As Ilan Berman, vice president of the American Foreign Policy Council in Washington rightly states, *"What we're looking at is not simply an economic play. It's an economic play that also has political and strategic undertones."*

III. BRAZIL & ARGENTINA: PROJECTING REGIONAL POWER

Brazil is the biggest defense spender in South America and number 12 in the world in terms of military expenditure[16]. The South American giant has an advanced nuclear energy program that dates back to the fifties which has been supported at different stages by France, Germany and the U.S. Brazil's nuclear energy program provides around 3% of its domestic electricity and, in view of its dependence on hydroelectric power, which accounts for 75 % of the total power generated in the country, the Brazilian government intends to expand it.

In 2008, President Lula, one of the founding fathers of Latin American *"Narcopopulism"* through the *Foro de Sao Paulo*, announced that Brazil's National Defense Strategy would include the development acquisition of a nuclear-powered submarine[17], as part of the country's new policy aimed at exerting control over its vast maritime areas and exhibiting power projection. The relevance and motives behind the costly project generated controversy both at the domestic and at the international level.

---

[16] Source: Stockholm International Peace Research Institute (SIPRI)
[17] A submarine is considered to be nuclear because of its propulsion system and not because it can carry nuclear missiles (BBC Mundo, August 4, 2011)

Argentina has been involved in the production of nuclear energy for several decades. The country has not only exported nuclear technology to neighboring countries but also to countries in other continents such as Algeria, Egypt and Australia. In August 2011, the Argentinian government declared that the country had plans to develop a nuclear-powered submarine, only a few days after Brazil had announced it would be building its own. Despite the fact that both countries emphasized that their plans did not have belligerent purposes, the development of a second submarine in the region led to conjectures by experts in relation to a possible regional *arms race*.

IV. VENEZUELA: THE TRAILBLAZER

One of Hugo Chávez's grand ambitions was converting the socialist *Bolivarian Republic* into a regional military power. Walking the talk, by the moment of his death, Chávez had taken important steps in that direction. A study by led by SIPRI mentions Venezuela as being the largest importer of conventional weapons to Latin America since the beginning of 21st century, and despite its economic collapse, the country still spearheads the regions military expenditures. According to data published on February 2016 by SIPRI, Venezuela occupies the 18th place in the list of the world's largest buyers of weapons and it has spent some US $ 5.62 billion in arm purchases between 1999 and 2015. The Sweden based institute refers to Venezuela having disbursed as much as US $ 162 million in 2015, out of which US $ 147 million would have gone to China.

The obvious question here is, how is a country with the world's highest inflation rates, whose economy shrank 8% and where the population is finding it hard to access basic food supplies able to sustain such an investment? Regrettably, this brings back to mind Kim Jong-un's Democratic People's Republic of Korea, where a costly nuclear program is developed even though millions of its inhabitants live in calamitous conditions.

V.   GOING ATOMIC

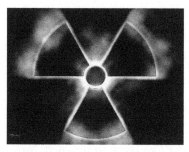

Latin American countries' heavy reliance on hydroelectric power led many of these to look for alternative energy sources, particularly as erratic climate patterns were rendering this type of energy less reliable. Countries like Brazil and Argentina have been aiming to triple their nuclear energy sources in order to generate electricity for their mammoth urban centers. Other countries such as Mexico, Chile, Uruguay and Venezuela have also embarked on major projects to build nuclear reactors.

Photo: Web

Then again, any matter that involves the use of nuclear energy must consider the disturbing possibility of it being used for purposes other than peaceful. Before Brazil's Lula and Venezuela's Chávez brought the nuclear issue to light, the possibility of countries in Latin America being involved in non-peaceful nuclear energy deals was remote. In February 2012, the UN Secretary General Ban Ki-Moon hailed the 40 years of the Treaty of Tlatelolco, a pact signed in 1967 for the prohibition of nuclear weapons in Latin America and the Caribbean. However, while this happened, the UN's own nuclear watchdog was pointing at the existence of nuclear energy programs for military purposes in various counties in the region. The main issue to be highlighted here though, is the aforementioned convergence of countries which hold deep animosity towards the U.S. amid the region's convoluted geopolitical juncture, which might ultimately translate into the end of the region's historical exclusion from the world's *nuclear club*.

V.1   THE TEHRAN-CARACAS NUCLEAR AXIS

Only a few years after taking seat, Hugo Chávez announced his intentions to develop nuclear energy in Venezuela in order to provide for the country's public energy requirements. Chávez's nuclear energy agenda was vigorously supported by countries such as Russia and Iran, with whom Venezuela had established strong military cooperation ties. In April 2008, Venezuela and Iran signed a military and defense cooperation agreement in which the two countries pledged to cooperate in the field of nuclear technology and alternative energy sources. In a public broadcast that followed the signature of the agreement, both heads of state joked about their intentions to produce *"a bomb"*, mocking US opposition to the development of nuclear energy by Iran. Chávez added that he had sent an official request to the IAEA for the *"Introduction of a Nuclear Energy Program"* in Venezuela.

Secret U.S. diplomatic cables, released by WikiLeaks, claimed that at least 57 Iranian specialists visited Venezuela in the past five years to prospect for uranium, needed for Tehran's controversial nuclear program.

V.2   THE RELENTLESS SEARCH FOR URANIUM

Uranium exploration, both legal and illegal, is in *vogue* in Latin America. Uranium deposits have been discovered in Brazil, Argentina, Colombia, Guyana, Paraguay and Peru, and while private investors have begun to realize the billions of dollars that Latin America's uranium deposits may represent, the Islamic Republic if Iran has also engaged into a relentless pursuit of the mineral across the region since 2006. Iran has incessantly sought uranium in Venezuela, Ecuador and Bolivia and has also tried to access Argentina's nuclear technology.

In October 2009, President Hugo Chávez announced that Iran and Venezuela were working together in the exploration and mining of uranium deposits in Venezuelan territory. Iran and Venezuela have allegedly set up joint front companies that are covertly mining uranium. According to financial crime expert, Kenneth Rijock, *"there are joint Venezuelan-Iranian aluminum mines in Venezuela that are most likely covertly mining uranium."* An announcement by the Venezuelan government forbidding air-traffic above the mines and forewarning that aircraft which flew over these would be shot down, heightened apprehensions. In the meantime, Chávez had proceeded to the arbitrary expropriation of lands where uranium deposits had been found.

According to a secret Israeli government report Venezuela and Bolivia are supplying Iran with uranium for its nuclear program

V.3 BOLIVIA'S NUCLEAR DREAMS

Bolivian President Evo Morales has been a central figure of Latin America 21st century *"narcopopulism"* and a strident advocate of *anti-US* sentiment in the region. As Venezuela's Chávez, Morales also forged close links with Iran, Russia and China which have all supported the modernization of the Bolivian military. Iran offered Bolivia its assistance in the development of a nuclear program, including the building of a nuclear plant using Iranian technology. Russia, from its side, committed to support Bolivia in the establishment of a *state-of-the-art* nuclear technology center in the city of El Alto, the first of its kind in the region. In turn, China has offered the Andean country a series of soft loans aimed at strengthening Bolivia's Navy, Army and Air Force.

As for allegations regarding Bolivia's involvement in uranium exploitation, dubious practices that closely mirror Iran's *modus operandi* in Venezuela have been surfacing. Amongst these is a joint venture between Bolivia, Iran and Venezuela to build a cement factory in the Andean Coroma zone, worth US $ 115 million. An investigation led by six U.S. scientists with NASA's support reported the existence of rich uranium, gold, silver and copper deposits in the mine's area. The Bolivian government has repeatedly denied the existence of uranium deposits in the country's territory.

"Several South American countries participate in a regional uranium exploration project."

Mohamed ElBaradei, former head of the International Atomic Energy Agency (IAEA)

V.4 KEEP AN EYE ON ECUADOR

Rafael Correa's Ecuador defense spending has been twice the size of the sum of military expenditures by the three previous governments. Besides an agreement signed with Russia in 2009 for Ecuador to develop a nuclear energy program, the Andean country has suspiciously embarked in the search of uranium in its soil. According to the former IAEA director, Mohamed El Baradei, Ecuador has been part of a *"regional"* uranium exploration initiative driven by Iran. U.S. authorities also reported that a US $ 30 million joint mining deal had been completed between Iran and Ecuador in December of 2009 had been brought to their attention. The government of Ecuador flatly denied the accusations through its embassy in Washington, saying it knew nothing about uranium deposits in the country.

"I am gravely concerned that Ecuador is solidifying its status as a willing accomplice to an Iranian agenda focused on harming the United States, our interests, and our allies. The United States must look closely at this unabashed cooperation and address Correa's potential role in assisting Iran's nuclear ambition."

US Senator Ileana Ros Lehtinen

V.5 NUCLEAR TERRORISM

One of the modern world's worst nightmares is that of a nuclear weapon falling in the hands of a terrorist organization. This fear grew in the early nineties, following the dissolution of the Soviet block of nations and the ensuing loss of control over its huge nuclear arsenal. Based on information which confirmed Al Qaeda's relentless pursuit of a nuclear device, the 2010 Nuclear Security Summit held in Washington D.C. focused on the issue of controlling potential access by terrorist groups to nuclear materials.

Al Qaeda has reportedly been seeking nuclear weapons since 1992, shortly after the end of the Cold War. The terrorist has allegedly attempted to buy stolen weapons and nuclear material in Russia and in several of the former Soviet republics. Information also surfaced on the training of Al Qaeda operatives by corrupt elements of the Pakistani nuclear program in the making of bombs capable of carrying nuclear warheads.

Another terrorist organization that has apparently been following the uranium trail is Colombia's FARC. In March 2008, Colombian authorities found a cache of 66 pounds of depleted uranium, presumably belonging to FARC, just outside Bogota. Uranium was also mentioned in recordings found in computers recovered after a raid by the Colombian Armed Forces on a FARC camp in Ecuador in 2008.

Following the November 2015 Paris attacks, Belgian authorities raided the home of a man with alleged ties to the Islamic State and discovered that video surveillance had been used to spy on a senior Belgian nuclear researcher. This raised suspicions in the sense that members of the extremist group were conceivably trying to obtain nuclear material to create a *"dirty bomb"*[18] to be used in a major European city, possibly by threatening or kidnapping the man or his family[19].

"We know that it would not require a team of nuclear physicists or even a particularly sophisticated criminal network to turn raw material into a deadly weapon...in many cases, a determined lone wolf or a disgruntled insider is all it might take."

Belgian Energy Department internal report – May 2013

In my view, nobody has been able to describe the true nature of the potential threat that nuclear terrorism represents better than Harvard University's Graham Allison. In his book, *The Ultimate Preventable Catastrophe*, the author strongly warns about the imminent and serious danger posed by nuclear terrorism today. According to Allison, there are two main reasons that make nuclear terrorism a threat of catastrophic dimensions. First, the growing evidence that terrorist groups like Al Qaeda and other criminal organizations have been trying to get hold of nuclear material and second, the availability of

---

[18] A "dirty bomb" is a radiological dispersal device that combines conventional explosives, such as dynamite, with radioactive material *(United States Nuclear Regulatory Commission)*
[19] Source: Center for Public Integrity

huge amounts of suitable material for the production of nuclear weapons which evades the control of national and/or international authorities. Allison denounces what he calls *"the loss of focus on a danger of unimaginable consequences."*

THE ATOMIC BOMB

Photo: U.S. Department of Defense

An atomic bomb or *a*-bomb is a weapon which derives its explosive force from the release of nuclear energy through the fission of heavy atomic nuclei. Isotopes uranium-235 and plutonium-239, which are both capable of undergoing a chain reaction, are the practical fissionable nuclei used in atomic bombs. In view of the fact that uranium-235 accounts for only 1% of natural uranium or Uranium-238, large amounts of the latter require to be converted using powerful centrifugal machines to produce minimal amounts of uranium-235.

VI. NATO: A DIFFERENT BALL GAME

In June 2013, the North Atlantic Treaty Organization (NATO) signed a security cooperation agreement with Colombia aimed at exchanging intelligence information in order to improve the capabilities to face common threats, particularly in the realm of transnational  organized crime. The agreement was considered an important step in improving cooperation between NATO and Latin American democracies. Upon being informed of the agreement several Latin American nations vigorously expressed their disapproval of NATO's interference in regional affairs in the usual *anti-US* inflammatory rhetoric calling it *"a threat to the region."* Amongst these, the most outspoken was the Brazilian government whose foreign policy efforts have sought to diminish U.S. influence in the region in order to reassert its role as a regional power.

However, amongst the most illustrative efforts to reduce U.S. prominence in the region, were those made by Colombia and Ecuador. On 30 October 2009, under former President Alvaro Uribe's government, Colombia and the U.S. had signed a military agreement which allowed the U.S. to make use of seven military bases on Colombian territory. As expected, Venezuela, Bolivia and Ecuador were quick to react against the deal. Only 10 months later, in August 2010, Colombia's Constitutional Court declared the agreement unconstitutional, claiming that under the Constitution, any new international treaty had to be transacted in Congress, a requirement which the agreement had not complied with.

In reaction to Colombia's Constitutional Court decision, the U.S. State Department said that it respected the decisions made by democratic institutions in Colombia. However, according to the Colombian newspaper *El Tiempo*, the U.S. expected President Juan Manuel Santos to push the agreement though congress, as he himself had negotiated the deal as defense minister. Unexpectedly, though, in what in retrospect constitutes Santos' first ambiguous move, he simply proceeded to acknowledge the Court's decision, avoiding any public statements on the matter.

In the same manner, in 2009, Ecuador's President Correa decided to close a U.S. military base that operated in the coastal city of Manta which had been playing a crucial role in the fight against drug trafficking. Since the closure of the base, cocaine smuggling has thrived all along Ecuador's Pacific Ocean coast[20].

Fogh Rasmussen, former NATO director said in 2012 that NATO had to adopt a global perspective, and that a global perspective meant being constantly aware of how global challenges affected the security of the alliance's members. However, serious doubts have arisen in regards to NATO's assessment of the growing threat that the new adverse dynamics of Latin American geopolitics represents. Since the time when the above mentioned anti-NATO statements were made, not only have *Bolivarian* nations gained greater control over the region, but links between European transnational crime and narcoterrorist organizations such as Colombia's FARC have intensified.

Furthermore, as we will see in Chapter 8, the possibility of Colombia turning into a full-fledged Narco-State under FARC's rule as a result of the government's shady **Peace Talks**, is not only real but also imminent. Should this be the case, and unless NATO's plans include joining hands with one of the world's largest narcoterrorist organizations in order to fight Transnational Organized Crime, the basic objective of the 2013 NATO-Colombia agreement will have been self-defeated.

In any case, regardless of how things evolve in convoluted Latin America, one thing remains certain. By merely uttering of the word "NATO", *Bolivarian* nations and their criminal cohorts enter into a **state of panic**. These know well that an active role by NATO in the region would translate into a *totally different ball game;* one in which their ghastly goals would be seriously challenged.

---

[20] Espinoza, Andrea. "La industria del narcotráfico se expande en Ecuador," El País, Internacional, 31/05/2012.

CHAPTER 5

THE NARCOPOPULIST OFFENSIVE

As mentioned in Chapter 3, the vacuum left by the US in its *backyard* led to the emergence of so called *"socialist"* governments throughout the region, steered by Brazil's Ignacio Lula da Silva and by Venezuela's late Hugo Chávez Frías. Lula da Silva piloted the infamous **Foro de Sao Paulo**, whose main objective is taking over Latin America and establishing *socialism* across the region. Chávez, on the other hand, inspired of 20th century Marxist ideology and by the Cuban revolution, introduced what he called **XXI Century Socialism**, and was soon followed by Rafael Correa in Ecuador, Evo Morales in Bolivia and Daniel Ortega in Nicaragua *(Argentina's Cristina Fernández de Kirchner was later drawn into the game by Chávez)*.

Aside from the *thruway* provided by the U.S. for these governments to surface, Latin America's persistent poverty and growing inequality constituted the ideal grounds for the populist discourse to thrive. In addition, the *socialist* sermon already included the necessary ingredients to denounce U.S. influence in the region, namely, the *anti-imperialistic* and *anti-capitalistic* creeds.

That Hugo Chávez managed to change the political dynamics of an entire region is a matter of fact. Chávez conquered the underprivileged masses of Venezuela, and his populist charisma and rhetoric attracted national and international attention. Beyond Chávez, *"Chavismo"* remains very much alive, to the extent that some Venezuelans literally venerate the late leader and have even built chapels in his honor.

A vocal *anti-US* advocate, Chávez established links with every possible U.S. foe in the planet. He opened Latin America's door to Iran, Russia and China which did not hesitate to mark a strong presence in the region. He defended Libya's

Gadhafi and Syria's Al Assad and called George W. Bush *the devil* in the UN general assembly. Nevertheless, the worst part of his legacy, were the connections he made with organized crime and drug trafficking, in particular by teaming up with Colombia's FARC and by providing Hezbollah and other Islamic terrorist organizations unimpeded access to the region.

While Hugo Chávez's populist appeal was undeniable, what actually underpinned his success was the unprecedented increase in world oil prices which reached levels above US $ 100 per barrel practically throughout his 16 years in power. Venezuela, an old member of the oil exporting club, has the largest oil reserves in the planet. The country's enormous oil riches coupled with the increasing availability of drug money, provided Chávez the ideal ingredients to further his cause in the national, regional and international arenas.

And money was indeed at the heart of Chávez's global public relations drive. According to the opposition, between 2005 and 2011, Chávez awarded at least US $ 82 billion in grants to more than 40 countries. The main beneficiaries of these grants were Cuba, Nicaragua, Argentina and Ecuador, but many other countries also profited from his *"generosity"*, including Syria, to which he reportedly sent US $ 10 million worth of oil. However, the aim of his *rapprochement* to some of the leaders of these countries was not always merely inducing these to join his cause. As previously mentioned, in Argentina's case, his close relationship with former president Cristina Fernández de Kirchner sought to allow Iran access to the country's nuclear technology.

I.   THE "FORO DE SÃO PAULO" *(The Sao Paulo Forum)*

The **Foro de São Paulo (FSP)**, is an alliance of *"leftist"* political parties and organizations from Latin America and the Caribbean. Founded in 1990 in the city of Sao Paulo by Cuba's Fidel Castro and former Brazilian President Ignacio Lula da Silva who used Brazil's PT Worker's Party (*Partido dos Trabalhadores*) as a platform, the forum brought together more than one hundred legal parties and several criminal organizations linked to the drug trafficking industry, such as Colombia's FARC. Formed in response to the end of Soviet Union's political and financial sponsorship of the Latin American *"left"*, the group has provided its members pivotal political and financial support in order to spread *socialism* across the region. By supporting politicians in various countries, FSP has influenced national electoral processes and has managed to place political figures in key positions, including several of the region's leaders.

However, amongst FSP's most disturbing ties were those it established with Colombia's FARC. In December 2001, under the chairmanship of Brazil's Lula da Silva, FSP emitted a manifesto in FARC's support, calling the Colombian government's actions against the terrorist group *"state terrorism."* Two years later, in March 2003, Brazil's PT Worker's Party refused to classify FARC as a terrorist organization, upon a request by the Colombian government. Despite irrefutable evidence pointing at FARC's contribution to the forum's undertakings, FSP officials have repeatedly denied any links with the narcoterrorist organization.

"Never before has the world seen such an intimate, persistent, organized and lasting coexistence between politics and crime, and on such a gigantic scale"

Olavo de Carvalho – Brazilian Writer

II.   THE SOMBER LEGACY

If these ever actually existed, the "noble" intentions of the FSP or, by the same token, of the so called **XXI Century Socialism**, rapidly vanished and degenerated into corruption, authoritarianism, brutal repression, gross human rights violations and in a severe crackdown on freedom of expression. Incipient democratic institutions, painstakingly built in the 20th Century, were torn apart while nepotism prospered and electoral fraud became practically endemic.

As a result of serious mismanagement and corruption in the public sector, and hardly hit by the plummeting of world oil prices and China's economic woes, Latin America's economy has taken a serious dive. According to a Reuters poll conducted in July 2015, "*economic growth in Latin America will continue at a modest pace*" and indeed, GDP growth predictions of the largest economies have suffered significant downswings resulting in the dwindling popularity of most of the region's leaders.

Under President Dilma Roussef, Lula da Silva's handpicked successor, **Brazil** is going through its lengthiest recession in decades. The country's economy is expected to contract 1.5 percent this year and inflation has reached levels of as much as 10%.

The economic model of **XXI Century Socialism** failed badly. Today, Venezuelan people live amid blackouts, food shortages, and rampant crime and corruption. The country's supermarkets are practically empty, breweries don't have enough barley, malt and other imported products required to make beer, and even toilet paper is scarce. **Venezuela** is essentially bankrupt. The IMF projects inflation will shoot up to 720% in 2016 and real gross domestic product, which contracted 10% in 2015, will probably contract 6% in 2016.

Venezuela, whose hard currency revenues depend around 96% on oil, was one of the most severely affected countries by the fall in world oil prices, and while other oil rich nations had been more cautious in regards to such an eventuality, the calamitous management of Venezuela's oil sector certainly didn't help. Operating at less than half capacity, poorly managed (Chávez had replaced oil professionals for his cronies) and with little or no maintenance of oil installations, oil production fell 25% between 1999 and 2013. State owned PDVSA (Petróleos de Venezuela, S.A.), is not only in shambles, but it has also been allegedly involved in obscure financial transactions worth millions of dollars.

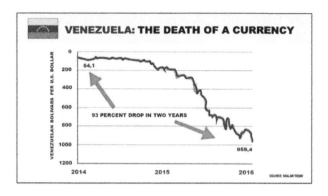

Argentina, one of the region's main economies, experienced eight long years of decay under former President Cristina Fernández de Kirchner. Kirchner's arbitrary and shady policies resulted in rampant insecurity and crime, weakened financial institutions and practically *divorced* the country from the global economy. According to a Barclays November 2015 report, as real incomes fall, the economy will shrink by 1.1% next year. The country posted a US $ 3 billion trade deficit in 2015 and, despite some optimism following the election of Mauricio Macri in November 2015, it will still have to tackle high inflation levels which reached 25% in 2015.

Rafael Correa's Ecuador, another oil rich nation which reaped the fruits of high oil prices during the past decade, did not escape the *Bolivarian* nations' demise. Correa, yet another fervent and vocal *anti-US* advocate, became increasingly authoritarian and, like his pairs, opened the door to drug trafficking and rampant corruption. Among his most reproachable deeds was his ruthless clamp down on the media which was, and continues to be, universally condemned.

The *"Ecuadorian Miracle"* was short-lived. Making good use of the customary XXI Century Socialism populist rhetoric and investing a hefty part of the country's oil money in a costly and impressive road network, Correa managed to deceive his people and the world in regards to what was apparently a thriving economy and a nation in the path of prosperity. However, it didn't take long for the world to realize that what actually lied behind the Ecuadorian leader's self-professed success were inordinate levels of public spending and, like in Chávez's case, the squandering of the country's oil wealth. Today, as a result of the fall of world oil prices, the country's economy is in dire straits.

Ecuador's main export is crude oil, which the Andean country exports mostly to Asia, the U.S. and the Caribbean. Gross economic mismanagement coupled with the sharp drop in commodities prices led the country to an unsustainable fiscal deficit. The level of public spending by the end of 2014 represented 44% of GDP and its total debt reached US $ 32 billion. China, which has become Ecuador's major lender since 2009, has recurrently been coming to the rescue. According to the *Financial Times*, the country's current debt with China stands at approximately US $ 5 billion[21].

"Something similar is happening in Ecuador. Over the last week, social unrest has spread throughout the country. Beneath the surface, the problem is much larger because the public knows that he government's retrograde economic policies are counterproductive"

Ezequiel Vázquez-Ger - Director of the Center for Investigative Journalism in the Americas

---

[21] As at November 2015

III. BOLIVIA'S COCAINE KINGDOM

Perhaps the most colorful of Latin America's present-day leaders is Bolivia's Evo Morales, whose strident *anti-imperialistic* statements have granted him international notoriety. However, in addition to his bombastic pronouncements, Morales has added a dose of amusement to the *"socialist"* creed, through sporadic preposterous remarks, including advice on refraining from eating chicken in order to avoid becoming a homosexual.

First elected in 2005, Morales renewed his mandate in 2009 and 2014 via doubtful election processes. Aside from following the authoritarian path of his *Bolivarian* partners, information on his alleged involvement in the cocaine business has emerged. According to the *EFE news agency*, a group of senior officials close to Morales is currently under investigation by U.S. authorities, based on information provided by a DEA informant.

RAFAEL CORREA: ECUADOR'S DRUG-STAINED

Ecuador's President **Rafael Correa** always denied any connections with Colombia's narcoterrorist organization FARC and vehemently rejected accusations about FARC's alleged drug-money contributions to his presidential campaign. However, Correa's categorical denial clashed with ample and irrefutable evidence to the contrary.

Information found in March 2008 FARC computers seized after a Colombian Armed Forces attack on a FARC camp which operated without restrictions in Ecuadorian territory, revealed close links between Correa's government and the narcoterrorist group, including communications that divulged that the Ecuadorian president received periodic reports about FARC's activities in the country (later confirmed by WikiLeaks). FARC's presence in Ecuador is indisputable. The narcoterrorist organization is involved in drugs, arms and human trafficking through corruption networks that involve both local authorities and the military. At a given point in time, FARC managed to operate 11 camps on Ecuadorian soil, close to its border with Colombia. There are even reports that indicate that FARC had been seen wearing Ecuadorian Army uniforms in the area.

As mentioned in Chapter 4, in 2009, Correa's decision to close a U.S. military base that operated in the coastal city of Manta resulted in inordinate growth of the cocaine business in Ecuador's Pacific Ocean coast.

Bolivia is now literally at the center of South America's illegal drug trade and it has partnered with Colombia's FARC to become the major supplier to the Brazilian and Argentine[22] cocaine consumer markets. Coca base *(also called cocaine paste)*, is delivered to organized crime syndicates[23] which then sell the finished product at the domestic level or export it to African and European markets. According to the military, under Morales Bolivia became the cocaine export base for Venezuela, Cuba, Libya, Iran and Russia. In 2008, Bolivia's Morales expelled the U.S. Drug Enforcement Agency (DEA), accusing it of meddling in national sovereignty matters.

"They are controlling coca leaf, but indications are that trafficking and transport of the drug are increasing."

Roberto Laserna, Bolivian economist - Fundación Milenio

In August 2015, the UN announced that Bolivia had reduced land planted with coca for the fourth consecutive year. Morales, who had himself o been a coca grower, had convinced unions to decrease the size of the annual coca crop. However, the president's detractors rapidly noted that the UN report only considered the coca leaf crop and left out crucial data on the amounts of coca leaf being transformed into cocaine. Bolivia's former "drug czar" Ernesto Justiniano cautioned that UN reports were based on data provided by the national government and that these required its approval prior to publication. He added that Bolivia's cocaine production now amounts to a 160 tons a year, twice the amount produced in 2008.

The White House Office on National Drug Control Policy reported that after declining from 2010 to 2012, Bolivian coca cultivation and production spiked again in 2014.

---

[22] Domestic drug consumption in Argentina has sky-rocketed in recent years

[23] Brazilian criminal organizations such as the notorious *Comando Vermelho* control drug sales in Sao Paulo and Rio de Janeiro and have stretched their business across Brazil.

IV. SPAIN'S PODEMOS: NARCOPOPULISM'S GATE TO EUROPE

In the fall of 2014, Spanish press reported that Spain's Pablo Iglesias, leader of the far-left party *Podemos,* had traveled to Bolivia to meet President Evo Morales. During his visit, and amid mutual adulations, Morales said that their shared desire was for Spain to become Bolivia's *door to Europe*.

Nothing wrong with the leaders of two countries meeting and sharing their affinities, however, according to information provided to Spanish police by a confidential DEA source, the governments of Iran and Venezuela had allegedly channeled funding to Spain's **Podemos** through a company controlled by a prominent Iranian businessman. Spanish media stated that the source of this information had been a former high-ranking Venezuelan government official.

While Spain's anti-money laundering authorities are still examining the evidence, if this information is confirmed, not only would **Podemos** have infringed Spanish law on the financing of political parties, but Europe's gate to *"narcopopulism"* will have indeed been opened.

V. A MULTILATERAL MESS

Throughout its modern history, Latin America had made several attempts to achieve multilateral integration between countries in the region and, while some of these have worked better than others, the Organization of American States (OAS) had customarily been the platform on which matters of regional interest were deliberated upon. This is no longer the case. As part of the *narcopopulist* governments' efforts to isolate the US in the region, Fidel Castro and Hugo Chávez supported the creation of new multilateral organs such as CELAC and UNASUR, which exclude the U.S. and Canada from their membership. The tangible outcome of these developments has essentially been the proliferation of politically-biased multilateral institutions in the region.

V.1 THE ORGANIZATION OF AMERICAN STATES - OAS

The first target of the region's *narcopopulist* governments was the OAS. Considered as one of the US's main foreign policy instruments, the OAS constituted a major obstacle to their political maneuvers. Furthermore, the fact that Cuba was not a member of the organization had been the object of repeated criticisms by most countries in the region[24]. Today, as new multilateral organs gain ground, the organization is being progressively ostracized, as clearly demonstrated by CELAC's involvement in Colombia's **Peace Talks**, which we will cover in further detail in Chapter 8. The OAS's future now largely depends on how relations between the U.S. and countries in the region evolve in the near future.

V.2 THE UNASUR

The Unión de Naciones Suramericanas UNASUR *(Union of South American Nations)* is an intergovernmental body whose stated objective is to enhance regional economic and political integration in South America. One of Lula's and Chávez's *"babies"*, UNASUR was created in 2008 and its lavish US $ 38 million headquarters were established in Ecuador's capital, Quito. The organization's members are Brazil, Colombia, Argentina, Chile, Peru, Ecuador, Bolivia, Guyana, Paraguay, Suriname, Uruguay and Venezuela.

In July 2004, Colombia's ex-president Ernesto Samper, a staunch *anti-US* advocate and an ally of Lula and Chávez, was appointed as UNASUR's Secretary General. Samper's dubious credentials include obscure links with the drug establishment since the time of his presidency between 1994 and 1998. The Colombian politician had allegedly accepted in excess of US $ 6 million from Colombia's Cali Cartel for his presidential campaign and despite solid evidence in that respect, the Colombian ex-president has always denied the allegations. However, as a result of the chaotic situation that ensued, the U.S. shunned Samper's government, annulled his visa and forbid him from entering the U.S.

---

[24] Cuba was suspended during the Cold War in 1962

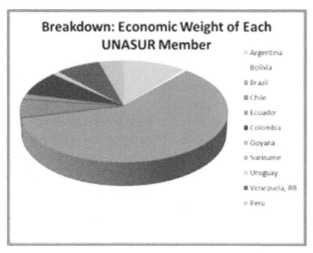

Source: AS/COA

To date, UNASUR's regional integration efforts have been mighty scarce and, under Samper, quite the opposite has actually transpired. UNASUR has become a public platform for *"socialist"* leaders to wash their dirty laundry and to launch verbal attacks against U.S. *"imperialist"* policies in the region further fragmenting an already disjointed region.

> *"UNASUR is born and the OAS has less to do every day,*
> *and now that it is divided, even less."*
>
> Hugo Chávez

V.3   CELAC

The Comunidad de Estados Latinoamericanos y Caribeños, CELAC *(Community of Latin American and Caribbean States)*, is a regional coalition of Latin American and Caribbean states created in 2010 in Mexico, whose aim is to promote the integration of countries in the region. Its creation represented a real source of pride for its members given the fact that, contrary to the OAS, it included Cuba and excluded the U.S. and Canada from regional discussions. In

CELAC's inaugural speech, Venezuela's Hugo Chávez defended what he called *"the battle for independence of the Latin American people from European powers and the US."*

In sum, Latin America's integration dreams are further away than ever before, and the vacuum of authentic multilateral governance has greatly contributed to mounting arbitrariness and to utter disrespect for international law. Coupled with the UN's inconsequential role in the region, Latin American people are now deprived of the right to resort to lawful supranational bodies.

VI.   THE REAL POWER BEHIND

Perhaps amongst the most relevant developments in 21st century Latin America is that alliances between countries have taken the lead over countries' individual stances. While ever improving communication technology has undeniably brought governments and people together, it is the purposeful and resolute effort of specific organizations and individuals that have driven the region's political course. As previously mentioned, three political figures lie at the origin of the dramatic change the region has undergone in recent years, namely, **Fidel Castro, Ignacio Lula da Silva** and **Hugo Chávez Frías**. However, a fourth actor which has played a vital role in terms of ensuring TOC's participation, has been Colombia's narcoterrorist organization **FARC**. As we will see in Chapter 7, U.S. and Europe's failure to appreciate this key geopolitical nuance lies at the root of the foreign policy fiasco *vis-à-vis* Latin America.

While Latin America's breakdown is most often attributed to Venezuela's Hugo Chávez (and there is little doubt that he is responsible for many of the region's afflictions), it was Cuba's Fidel who actually took advantage of U.S. absence in the region. Not only had Fidel Castro closed ranks with Lula da Silva to give birth to the powerful and influential **Foro de Sao Paulo**, but it was also the Cuban dictator who underpinned Hugo Chávez's **XXI Century Socialism** since its inception.

Shrewdly capitalizing on the fact that the Cuban revolution had been among Chávez's main sources of inspiration, Castro managed to remedy Cuba's post-

Cold War funding orphanage by persuading Chávez to provide Cuba billions of dollars in subsidized oil shipments and in investments in its oil infrastructure. According to some estimates, between 2008 and 2011, Venezuela transferred some US $ 18 billion to Cuba

But things didn't stop there. Apparently unsatisfied with the *life-line* the late Venezuelan president had extended, Castro decided to go for the whole deal. By astutely manipulating the country's new unskilled leader Nicolás Maduro, Castro literally took Venezuela over during a popular uprising against the government in February 2014. Cuban troops were transported to the country to provide support to Venezuela's repressive security apparatus, while government officials and Cuban agents took charge of some of the country's key institutions. For all intents and purposes, today's Venezuela is under Cuban control.

Both Castro and Chávez were instrumental in engaging FARC in their regional plans. Equally inspired by Cuba's revolution, FARC's access to the Caribbean island as a trampoline for drug trafficking in the Caribbean was certainly not problematic. Moreover, in his book *"Peace in Colombia"*, Fidel reveals his links with FARC's High Command and includes pictures of his meetings with the group's leaders. As we will see in Chapter 8, upon looking closer at Colombia's **Peace Talks** which *coincidentally* take place in Havana, Fidel's incidence goes well beyond merely hosting the talks and apparently involves President Santos's connivance.

Hugo Chávez never hid his sympathy for Colombia's FARC and the narcoterrorist organization was a crucial component of his *"Great Bolivarian Dream"*, one which would unite several countries into one sole grand nation as Simon Bolivar had done[25]. Considering that Colombia, which was one the U.S.'s closest allies in the region, was the only missing piece in the *Bolivarian* puzzle, Chávez considered FARC one of his most important strategic allies. According to Colombian authorities, Chávez provided millions of dollars to FARC in order to counterbalance the military power of Colombia's Armed Forces and had plans to rely on the narcoterrorist group to invade Colombia (see box). In addition, Chávez consented to FARC's total freedom of movement within Venezuelan

---

[25] Simón Bolívar "El Libertador" *(The Liberator)* was a military figure who played a key role in South America's fight for independence from Spain. Bolívar's victories led to the creation of the "Gran Colombia" in 1821, a federation of countries that included Venezuela, Colombia, Ecuador, Peru and Bolivia.

territory, supported the narcoterrorist group's drugs and arms trafficking activities, and lobbied on its behalf in international fora.

THE GUAICAIPURO "WAR" PLAN

Chávez regarded Colombia as a threat to Venezuela's national security. In 2008, Colombian authorities discovered that the late Venezuelan president had planned to invade Colombia with the help of other Latin American countries. The *"Guaicaipuro Plan"* had been specifically designed to launch a synchronic attack on Colombia with the help of Ecuador and Nicaragua, by making use of three different flanks. Venezuela was charge through Colombia's eastern border while Nicaragua and Ecuador would lead an assault through the Caribbean and the country's southern border, respectively. The plan's final goal, once the Colombian government had been toppled, was the establishment of a provisional government run by FARC.

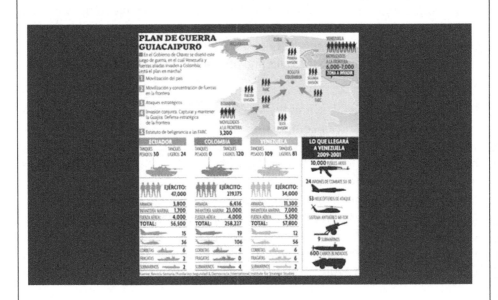

VIII. NARCOPOPULISM

If somebody is able to conclude that the information provided here above resembles in any manner the conventional meaning of *"socialism"*, we clearly need to hold a serious discussion. Far away from the 20th century cleavages that the so called *"socialist"* leaders insist in reviving, the sad spectacle Latin American democracies are going through is new, unprecedented and pertains <u>only</u> to the 21st century. It is undeniable that these leaders have done a brilliant job in terms of using *"socialism"* as a cover for their unscrupulous plans and have cunningly used the subterfuge to legitimize their governments before the international community. Nevertheless, what actually lies behind this curtain, is an amorphous association of drugs, terrorism and corruption whose sole purpose is to cling onto power and to ensure thereby the required conditions to keep their criminal enterprise afloat. The so called **XXI Century Socialism** is, hence, nothing more than a foul sophism of distraction which, aside from its cheap populist rhetoric has little, if anything, to do with Marxist or *"socialist"* ideology.

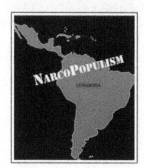

EL PLAN MAESTRO
OPINIÓN E INFORMACIÓN
INDEPENDIENTE

OCTOBER 04 2016

NARCO-POPULISM
LATIN AMERICA'S ONLY REAL ENEMY

"**Latin American** twenty-first century political phenomenon which operates under the cover of *"socialism or communism"* - whose sole objetive is seizing power by means of electoral fraud and force – backed by **International Drug Trafficking** and widespread **corruption**."

CHAPTER 6

FARC: CORPORATE NARCOTERRORISM

After a long cold shower in order to wash off the Somali desert dust, I joined a group of colleagues with whom I had agreed to meet in the lobby of the modest hostel where we were all staying. We had all worked hard since early in the morning in one of southern Somalia's hottest zones. Our team had been deployed with the intention of convincing local warring parties to provide free passage for much needed humanitarian aid.

When I entered the lobby, I couldn't help but noticing an expression of perplexity in my colleagues' faces as these were all attentively watching the old TV set placed in the middle of the room, over a worn out Persian-like carpet. Upon getting closer to the screen I saw disturbing images of men in cages in deplorable human conditions which instantly brought to mind the atrocities of the Nazi regime and thus led me to ask whether the images were from Nazi Germany. To my surprise, they all responded almost at unison *"It's Colombia, it's your country."* One of them added a comment which has stuck to my mind ever since: *"Man, your country is worse than Somalia!"*

And that was indeed what the images portrayed. My colleagues were watching a documentary film about FARC which illustrated the appalling level of brutality of the Colombian narcoterrorist organization. The film showed the way in which FARC kept its *"prisoners of war"* in cages, in the middle of amazon jungle, in the most appalling and infrahuman conditions. Many of the prisoners had been there for several years and some were kept permanently chained. The skeleton-like condition of most of the captives clearly indicated that these had hardly been fed.

A FARC operational manual found by Colombian authorities in November 2011 contained detailed instructions on hostage management: *"Prisoners should be monitored twenty-four hours a day and the most dangerous ones should be permanently chained... if there happens to be a surprise attack by the enemy, all prisoners must be immediately executed."* Other manuals found by local authorities dealt with extortion, landmines and with the use of dynamite to blow up bridges and electrical towers. *"If you decide to blow up a bridge you should first inform the local community about it. However, if there are cars or people on the bridge at the moment of the explosion...bad luck for them"*, said one of the manuals.

Photo: Web

FARC Prisoners

"People talk sometimes of a bestial cruelty, but that's a great injustice and insult to the beasts; a beast can never be so cruel as a man, so artistically cruel."

Fyodor Dostoyevsky

I. THE REVOLUTIONARY ARMED FORCES OF COLOMBIA: FARC

The Revolutionary Armed Forces of Colombia or FARC is an international narcoterrorist organization which has been at the center of a bloody confrontation that has wreaked havoc in Colombia for more than 50 years. Its origins date back to the early sixties, when *proxy* wars between the U.S. and the Soviet Union were ravaging Latin America and leftist guerilla groups sprouted across the region. FARC was founded by Jacobo Arenas in 1964, inspired by the Marxist revolutionary and anti-imperialist ideals of Fidel Castro's Cuban Revolution. Its main goal was the removal of Colombia's capitalist regime and the establishment of a Marxist-socialist regime. However, once the Cold War was over, FARC suffered a drastic transformation. The 20th century leftist revolutionary group gradually converted into one of the largest multinational narcoterrorist organizations in the world and, despite the fact that its ideology and revolutionary ideals have long disappeared, the organization continues to make shrewd use of its historical past as a cover to run its lucrative illicit business.

At present, FARC leads one of the largest drug trafficking networks in the world. It controls about 30% of Colombia's territory, particularly in the jungles of the south-east of the country, where coca plantations abound. According to the U.S. Department of Justice, FARC is responsible for more than 50% of global cocaine trade and for 60% of cocaine trafficked into the U.S.

FARC has a defined structure with a *central command* or *Secretariat* composed of 25 members. It is divided into geographical "blocks" made up of more than 50 "fronts." It counts on a solid support network which includes the best paid experts in a variety of areas associated to its highly diversified criminal activities. Besides drug trafficking, which remains the organization's core business, FARC is also involved in arms trafficking, illegal mining of minerals[26], kidnapping and extortion. In addition, FARC launders sizeable amounts of money through *"legal"* investments in key areas of the economy of various countries.

---

[26] The Colombian government estimates that one third of FARC's illegal income comes from illegal mining of minerals, especially gold and coltan.

In October 1997 the US State Department designated the FARC as a Foreign Terrorist Organization (FTO)

According to Colombian authorities FARC controls 60% of the country's drug trafficking and it holds the monopoly of opium poppy cultivation. The terrorist group is involved in all the phases of the drug operation including the cultivation of coca leaf, the production of high purity grade cocaine and the export of the final product to the U.S. and Europe. Most of the criminal organization's "fronts" are directly involved in the cultivation and production of cocaine and opium latex.

While towards the end of former President Alvaro Uribe's government in 2010 FARC's military capability had been significantly diminished, under President Juan Manuel Santos's rule the narcoterrorist organization has not only had the chance to reorganize and rearm, but it has also taken advantage of **Peace Talks** held in Cuba since November 2012 in order to increase its cocaine and heroin exports under scant restrictions.

All of FARC's Secretariat members are requested in extradition by the U.S. on drug charges.

FARC's enormous wealth makes of it one of the best armed terrorist groups in the world. Its military arsenal is composed of weapons from at least 25 different countries including Venezuela, Ecuador, Brazil, Russia, North Korea and Iran. As previously mentioned, FARC has also established links with Islamic extremist groups and African governments with whom it usually enters into drugs-for-weapons deals.

According to journalist Juanita León from Colombia's *La Silla Vacía*, a news website focused on Colombian politics, army estimates in 2012 revealed that FARC had 8,147 guerrilla fighters and 10,261 militiamen in camouflage in support networks, for a total of some 20 thousand people in arms. Within these support networks there were an additional 10,000 unarmed individuals (mostly the fighter's families), that provided food and shelter and alerted them if and when the army was close by. While some analysts have argued that the reduction in the number of FARC's troops indicated FARC's decline prior to the **Peace Talks** and that this was amongst the reasons that led the narcoterrorist group to sit at the table, not only has the narcoterrorist organization taken the upper hand in the negotiations, but it has also arrogantly and overtly affirmed that its main objective is, and has always been, to seize power. Moreover, it has had ample time to rebuild its military muscle since the prolonged talks began in 2012[27], and has been reportedly acquiring much more sophisticated weaponry than before.

Photo: Flickr Commons

FARC Child Soldier

"When it comes to indiscriminate murder, the Islamic State has nothing on the Revolutionary Armed Forces of Colombia (FARC). The Colombian terrorist group is every bit as cruel, and they've been at it for more than a half century", says *Wall Street Journal*'s Mary Anastasia O'Grady. While this is certainly a good attempt to describe FARC's viciousness, only the narcoterrorist group's more than 220,000 victims would have been able to tell the true story. FARC's crimes include extrajudicial killings, sexual abuse and forced abortion, recruitment of child soldiers, bomb attacks, planting of anti-personnel mines, forced displacement and violence against Christian communities and indigenous

---

[27] Among president Santos's main promises upon launching Peace Talks with FARC in 2012, was that these were had been planned to last a maximum of one year.

populations. According to the *International Campaign to Ban Landmines* (ICBL), *"FARC is probably the most prolific rebel group in the use of landmines in the world today."* The report in which this statement was published also mentioned that FARC generally assigned the planting of landmines to new forcibly recruited children.

"Colombia ranks third in the world for internally displaced people. Over four million Colombians are internally displaced due to narcoterrorism"

Consultancy on Human Rights and Displacement (CODHES)."

Although the underground and illicit nature of the criminal underworld makes it difficult for estimates to be accurate, according to several sources FARC has an annual turnover of about $ 600 million from drug deals alone. A 2014 *Forbes* report mentioned FARC as being the world's third richest terrorist organization, after ISIS and Hamas.

I.1 FARC & TRANSNATIONAL TERRORIST GROUPS

FARC's irruption into the realm of Transnational Organized Crime was probably part of the "natural" evolution of any expanding global business. Over time, the organization became the sponsor and coordinator of an intricate criminal network composed of terrorist and drug trafficking groups from across the region. Through this underground network FARC has been able to buy chemicals for the production of cocaine and other drugs, launder huge amounts of money and obtain *state-of-the-art* weaponry in exchange for drugs.

While it is obvious that FARC's business interests and that of the notorious Mexican Cartels overlap and makes their ties inevitable, these are also purposeful and intentional. Some have even referred to the existence of a *macro-cartel* which would be responsible for regulating global drug and arms trafficking in a concerted manner. Colombia's former Police Chief José Leon Riaño, confirmed FARC's strong ties to various Mexican drug cartels including the Sinaloa Cartel, the Tijuana Cartel and the Zetas. In view of the connections of Mexican cartels with drug trafficking organizations in Turkey, Iran and

Afghanistan, these ties have resulted in FARC's growing involvement in heroin trafficking.

While FARC's transnational criminal links primarily serve the purpose of drug trafficking, these have also profited from the *technical assistance* of other terror organizations that operate in the ambit of international terrorism. A few years ago, FARC's links with the Spain and France based *Euskadi Ta Askatasuna* (ETA) and with the *Irish Republican Army* (IRA), came to light. As previously mentioned, FARC also established links with Islamic extremist organizations such as Hezbollah and Al Qaeda, with the purpose of smuggling drugs into Europe through the African route.

Colombia's National Center for Historical Memory estimates that guerrilla groups kidnapped twenty-five thousand people between 1970 and 2010.

I.2   FARC'S PLANETARY SPREAD

Whereas the revolutionary activities of 20th century FARC were confined to the Colombian territory and focused exclusively on toppling the country's government, the tentacles of the 21st century narcoterrorist organization do not only spread to every corner of Latin America, but actually reach every corner of the planet. FARC's international criminal connections involve the establishment of logistical bases in various countries to run its drug business and the laundering of billions of dollars through the international financial and banking system. In addition, FARC's disquieting penetration into the highest levels of government of many Latin American and African countries has discernibly augmented.

Brazilian newspaper *O Estado de Sao Paulo* reported some years ago that FARC had established permanent bases in the jungles of northern **Brazil** in order to coordinate its drug and arms trafficking activities.

In March 2012, Panamanian security forces discovered and destroyed two FARC camps in **Panama**'s Darien region. The camps, which were camouflaged by the jungle's dense vegetation, were used by FARC's 57th Front, one of the richest and most powerful amongst the organization fronts. According to a US Treasury Department report, FARC money would have entered the Panamanian financial system through several companies and corporations

FARC controls much of **Peru**'s drug trafficking and is considered the main culprit behind the resurrection of *Sendero Luminoso*, a leftist insurgent group which had virtually disappeared under the rule of former President Fujimori. Its participation in the training of *Mapuche* militant groups in **Chile** was also confirmed by Colombian Police in May 2010.

And we haven't finished. FARC has reportedly also been involved in illegal mining activities in mineral rich **Guyana**. An *InSight Crime Analysis* report on the subject referred to FARC's activities in the Venezuelan border town of Santa Elena de Uairén. Just across the Brazilian and Guyanese borders, Santa Elena has become a strategic transit point for international illicit diamonds traffic. FARC's activities in the area allegedly include the transfer of illegal mining technology and of the *know-how* acquired by the organization back in Colombia.

And if any doubt remains in regards to FARC's global scope, computers seized following an attack launched by Colombia's government against a FARC camp in **Ecuador** in March 2008 revealed that the organization was also present in **Mexico, Argentina, Dominican Republic, Uruguay, Costa Rica, Paraguay, Spain, France, the UK, the Netherlands, Italy, Libya, Turkey** and even as far as **Australia**.

I.3 THE ALL-IMPORTANT CHÁVEZ-VENEZUELA CONNECTION

Hugo Chávez was instrumental in FARC's growth and expansion as an international criminal organization. Besides hosting FARC and allowing it to base its operations in Venezuelan territory, Chávez facilitated and funded FARC's arm deals in an effort to strengthen the group's capabilities to confront the Colombian Armed Forces which were primarily funded by the U.S. under "Plan Colombia."[28]

---

[28] "Plan Colombia" is a United States military and diplomatic aid package aimed at combating Colombian drug cartels and left-wing insurgent groups within Colombia's territory.

The late Venezuelan president was also the main link between FARC and Middle East Islamic terrorist groups. Amongst other efforts to tighten their cooperation, the government of Venezuela issued Venezuelan passports to senior FARC members for these to travel to the Middle East in 2006 in order to hold direct talks with Hezbollah in southern Lebanon. That same year, FARC provided fake documents to citizens of Egypt, Pakistan, Syria, Iraq and Jordan.

In 2009, Hugo Chávez decided to freeze relations with Colombia due to what he called an "aggression" by the Colombian government. Colombia had revealed the confiscation of weapons of Swedish origin which had originally been sold to the Venezuelan government.

But, paradoxically, it was Chávez's absence which actually led to much closer links between FARC and Venezuela. The political vacuum left by Chávez, which his successor Nicolás Maduro has noticeably been unable to fill, was occupied by FARC who transferred its command center to Caracas, where FARC's Supreme Leader alias Timoleón Jiménez *"Timochenko"* is currently based. And while FARC's drug trafficking ties with Venezuela date back more than a decade, under the new government and, capitalizing on the country's chaotic situation, FARC has been able to operate at ease, amid the *Bolivarian* Narco-State's drug-saturated political atmosphere. Moreover, an unholy and conspicuous multilateral relationship between Cuba's Castro, Venezuela's Maduro, Colombia's Santos and FARC has been developing which, as we will see in Chapter 8, illustrates how the Obama administration's inability to *grasp* the actual dynamics of this and other mischievous affiliations in the region has been at the forefront of the U.S. foreign policy failure in its *backyard*.

CHAPTER 7

THE WEST'S FLAWED APPROACH

If once there were green fields, now there is a *red backyard*. The map below illustrates the U.S.'s declining influence in Latin America and the Caribbean in the 21st century.

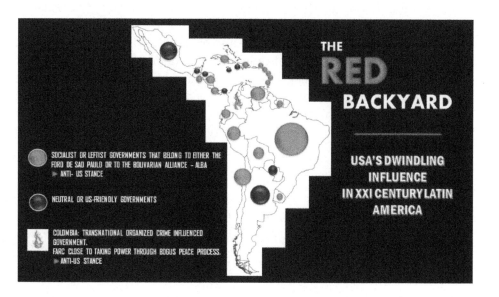

One thing is clear, the preponderant weight that the United States exerted over Latin America in the 20th century has come to an end. This outcome has been both the result of U.S. inattention, which has led to the weakening of democratic governance across the region, and to the assertive steps taken by those who have challenged Washington's historical weight in the region. If somebody ever dreamt of the economic integration of the Americas and of the creation of a powerful global economic bloc in the Western Hemisphere, this dream is visibly over.

It's rather obvious that the U.S. *"hands off"* approach to Latin America during the 90's led to the emergence of *anti-US* regimes in the region. However, it was the 11 September 2001 attacks on the U.S. that constituted the real turning point in the new relationship. Since that date, U.S. attention focused primarily on its challenges in the Middle East, while Latin America practically disappeared from its radar. This provided ample time for unfriendly and sinister alliances to mature and bred the enabling environment for their plans to materialize.

A few years later, when President Barack Obama's came to power, a region that aspired to consolidate its incipient democracies was optimistic in regards to what seemed to be a new levelheaded U.S. lead. However, if things had already been changing unfavorably, Obama's administration certainly made things worse. On the basis of the U.S.'s highly criticized interference in the region in the 20th century, not only did he decide not to *"meddle"* in regional affairs in spite of disturbing developments, but he also proceeded to restore ties with the Cuban regime - the main culprit of Latin America's demise and a major sponsor of terrorism and drug trafficking. While behind these decisions there must have been a Barack Obama that was either oblivious or confused in regards to Latin America's new reality, the celebration of his re-election by *"socialist"* leaders across the region *(who saw a Republican Party victory as a major threat)*, proved not to be gratuitous.

"The days in which our agenda in this hemisphere presumed that the United States could meddle with impunity, those days are past"

US President Barack Obama

I.   CUBA: A SHOT IN THE FOOT

"You want to consolidate our leadership and credibility in the hemisphere? Recognize that the Cold War is over. Lift the embargo", said Barack Obama during the 2015 State of the Union address, after having unexpectedly announced in December 2014 that America would restore diplomatic ties with Cuba.

It was clear that U.S. policy *vis-à-vis* Cuba, and in particular its five-decade-old blockade, was outdated and had proven to be increasingly counterproductive in regards to U.S. engagement with Latin America. Beyond the obvious, however, the challenge resided on how best to approach the matter, bearing in mind US National Interest and specially, U.S. National Security. Considering Cuba's central role in the disturbing political dynamics that has evolved in the region, it is difficult to comprehend how restoring ties with the Cuban Dictatorship can contribute to either of these. Moreover, what actually seems to transpire, is a gullible approach to resolving U.S. tribulations in the region by shaking hands with the Cuban Dictator.

The assumption that closer financial ties between the U.S. and Cuba will help to promote political reform in the country is both far-fetched and risky. Far-fetched because the chances that the longest-running dictatorship in the Western Hemisphere, whose brutality is amply documented, will candidly open up to promote democracy and human rights are very slim. Highly risky, because by propping up the morally bankrupt regime and enhancing its legitimacy the U.S. is essentially fueling the mischievous plans of the communist regime and its cohorts in the region and overseas. There's little doubt in my mind that amongst those who applauded the reestablishment of U.S. ties with Cuba were Iran, Russia and China and Colombia's FARC. Their unconditional and historical ally in the region had suddenly been given a chance to revive by no one else than their mutual opponent! And indeed, Obama's controversial initiative couldn't have been more opportune for the Cuban regime, in view of the fact that Venezuela (Castro's new benefactor), had collapsed and it was no longer in a position to rescue the island from an impeding economic crisis. As various members of congress said, Obama threw the mischievous Cuban regime an economic *lifeline*[29].

---

[29] Throughout its history, Castro's Cuba has been reliant on external sources in order to subsist. In what some call a *"parasitic dependence"*, the island has successively hinged on the US, the USSR and Venezuela to subsist.

The Obama administration said the rapprochement between the U.S. and Cuba would *"empower the Cuban people to decide their own future."* This was unsurprisingly questioned by pro-democracy and human rights activists as abuses and suppression of free speech and political repression have not eased. U.S. Republicans Marco Rubio and Ted Cruz, both sons of Cuban immigrants, harshly criticized Obama's move, maintaining that political change should have been a compulsorily prerequisite. And while some have argued that easing tensions and an eventual lift of a U.S. trade embargo Cuba would constitute a *win-win* scenario for the two countries, they tend to forget that the timeworn state-run economy is practically entirely under Raúl Castro's control, on whom the U.S. must rely for the required business-enabling changes to take place.

"We're not looking at a large impact on Cuba...for the U.S. economy, changes will be minimal"

Christopher Sabatini, Americas Society and Council of the Americas

The European Union (EU), on its side, either decided to mirror the U.S. approach to Cuba, or it coincidentally shares the Obama administration's obliviousness in regards to the regime's accountability for more than 50 years of crime and despotism. The EU also opted for restoring ties with Cuba, allegedly seeking a more constructive approach to engage Havana and to motivate President Raúl Castro's government to sign binding international human rights treaties.

The Political Dialogue and Cooperation Agreement (PDCA), reached by the parts on March 11, 2016, includes several trade components and also aims at *"promoting dialogue and cooperation to foster democracy and human rights and finding common solutions to global challenges."* However, while European foreign policy Chief Federica Mogherini has highlighted the issue of human

---

During the 90s, between the end of the Cold War and the providential advent of Hugo Chávez, Cuba had been unable to find alternative funding sources and fell into what Castro called a *"special period"*, forewarning the Cuban population about the difficulties the country was undergoing.

rights as being *a delicate matter* that needs to be addressed, failing to refer to Castro's accountability for decades of brutal repression provides the regime with undue legitimacy and unjustifiable impunity. Then again, the EU's *"constructive"* approach to Cuba, through which it expects the fifty-year-old brutal dictatorship to change its ways, aside from being somewhat credulous, disregards the detrimental role Cuba is currently playing throughout the Latin American subcontinent.

I.1   THE DISTURBING SPECTER OF IMPUNITY

An awkward tendency to consider Fidel Castro a *quixotic* character or to feel romantic about the *"Cuban Revolution"* has puzzlingly prevailed during many years. Those who maintain these views are either unacquainted with Cuba's dismal reality under Castro's rule, or they are simply indifferent to the suffering of thousands of human beings tortured, imprisoned or slain by the cold-blooded dictatorship. It is hard to find any other explanation to the incongruity of legitimating the cruelest and despotic regime in the history of the Western Hemisphere.

"The normalization of relations will embolden the Castro regime to continue its illicit activities, trample on fundamental freedoms, and disregard democratic principles."

US Senator Ileana Ros-Lehtinen

However, besides the damaging impact of ignoring the Cuban regime's appalling reality, what millions of Latin Americans deeply resent is the abominable impunity that this apathy entails. That heinous crimes systematically perpetrated by the Castro brothers during more than five decades will remain unpunished is not only objectionable, but it also sets a prejudicial precedent at a time when Cuba-inspired autocrats proliferate across the region.

In the same vein, when Latin America was informed that Pope Francis had issued a personal appeal to President Obama and to Cuba's President Raúl Castro for the *rapprochement* between the two nations to materialize, millions of

Catholics throughout the region reacted by condemning the Pope's promotion of his personal *leftist* political agenda at the expense of Castro's impunity, and of the tragic fate of thousands of his victims.

Perhaps one of the most troubling comments made by Barack Obama in this context was the one that referred to the need to *"recognize that the Cold War was over."* While some may see it as simple political rhetoric, the comment actually carries much greater significance than one would imagine. On the one hand, it gives the impression that the strategic analysis that underpins U.S. policy in Latin America is ill-informed, obsolete and hence, fundamentally flawed. Not only were the region's *"socialist"* governments and parties quick to reckon that the Cold War was over, but, as seen in previous chapters, these also made cunning use of the 20th century paradigm to conceal their ill-intentioned plans. On the other hand, the apparently simplistic understanding of geopolitical developments that transpired in the region during the last decade, suggests that it is Barack Obama who hasn't fully recognized that the Cold War is - in actual fact - over.

According to the Cuban Observatory on Human Rights, arbitrary arrests and detentions in Cuba climbed steadily throughout 2015 and hit 1,474 people in January 2016.

CHAPTER 8

COLOMBIA'S DRUG-TAINTED "PEACE"

THE LAST NAIL IN THE COFFIN

"But what do your Peace Talks have to do with us here in America?", asked a good American friend of mine some months ago after I had expressed my concerns about his country's future and disturbing developments in the U.S. *backyard*. Besides telling him *grosso modo* what has been revealed in this book thus far, I asked him: *"Did you ever think that US withdrawal from Iraq, some 6000 miles away, would lead to the birth of ISIS and would later translate into one of the biggest terrorist threats to the West today? Well, just imagine a much more vicious and equally ill-intentioned terrorist group, allied with US foes such as Iran and Hezbollah, but just across the US border."*

Two issues emerge here. First, as evidenced first by the 9/11 attacks and more recently by the ISIS attacks in Europe and in San Bernardino, terror has truly gone global, and it has reached U.S. and European soil. Second, this new phenomenon is the result both of a short-sighted foreign policy that has failed to understand 21st century geopolitical developments, and of a misplaced "politically correct" dogma which has been capitalized upon by "politically incorrect" parties.

Let me put it bluntly. Colombia's drug-tainted **Peace Talks** with narcoterrorist organization FARC are the last nail in the coffin in the context of the burial of America's control over its *backyard*. In other words, halting these constitutes the very last chance for the United States to prevent what slowly depicts itself as the gravest ever threat in its 240 year history.

It was in November 2012 that Colombia's President Juan Manuel Santos, out of the blue, opened **Peace Talks** with narcoterrorist organization FARC. The purported objective of the talks to be held in Havana, Cuba, was to put an end to a 50-year-old blood-stained confrontation between FARC and the Colombian State that had left more than 220,000 dead and had displaced more than 6 million people.

The unexpected announcement caught many by surprise. On the one hand, Santos had solemnly promised his electoral base to maintain his predecessor's fight against terrorism which had led to the serious weakening of FARC. On the other hand, the choice of Castro's Cuba for the talks to be held and of *Bolivarian* Venezuela as a *guarantor*, led millions of Colombians to question the president's genuine intent. Furthermore, an ambiguous agenda which left out key matters such as FARC's TOC connections and its links with Middle East Islamic terrorist groups, made things even less reassuring.

The **Peace Process**, meant to last one year *(now running through its 4th year)*, has not only been full of anomalies from the start, but it has also been ostensibly favoring FARC in almost every respect. FARC has rearmed[30], entered into drugs for weapons deals with Al Qaeda[31], violated ceasefires, maintained ferocious attacks against Colombia's armed forces, planted more mines and, more importantly, it has exported drugs and expanded it criminal enterprise practically unhindered under the banner of "Peace." In November 2015, the U.S. State Department's Bureau of International Narcotics and Law Enforcement noted that Colombia had once again become the world's largest exporter of cocaine.

If the above mentioned inconsistencies may seem familiar in the context of other unsuccessful peace attempts in other parts of the world, Colombia's talks with FARC have displayed an even more unsettling facet, fraught with outright absurdity, bordering *Kafkaism*. To be specific, FARC has barefacedly denied its involvement in drug trafficking, refused to admit its atrocities, publicly

---

[30] According to *InSight Crime Analysis*, the Ecuadorian military in charge of the border area of Colombia and Ecuador said that buying and arms trafficking had increased since the beginning of the Peace Process in Colombia.

[31] In March 2013, the US Drug Enforcement Agency (DEA) detained two FARC members in Algiers who were closing a drugs-for-weapons deal with elements form Al Qaeda in the Maghreb.

announced it will not lay down its weapons and negated the existence of billions in illicit drug money. However, there are still more fundamental pitfalls to this obscure initiative led by Colombia's equally obscure President Santos.

For international security expert Joseph Humire, Iran would be poised to fund FARC after signing the peace agreement with the Colombian government.

I.   WAR

Evidently, for there to be peace there must first be war, and in Colombia there is no war. There's war in Syria - where hundreds of missiles and dozens of warplanes incessantly bombard the Syrian population. There's war in Syria - where entire cities are demolished and where a myriad of terrorist groups fight relentlessly for power. Pretending that the crimes and barbarity perpetrated by a drug cartel such as FARC against the Colombian State constitute a "war" is a grave misjudgment. What Colombia has been suffering from during the past decades is a very serious problem of *law & order* caused by a criminal group that has been threatening democracy and the very existence of the State. The bulk of FARC's 220,000 victims have died in rural areas, where the narcoterrorist organization has hidden from State authorities, planted vast fields of coca leaf and poppy plants and managed its international criminal enterprise. As we will see further ahead, this problem has been exacerbated by immoderate permissiveness and impunity on the part of President Santos' government since the Havana-based talks began, in 2012.

II.   PEACE & LEGITIMACY

Never before has the *sacrosanct* concept of "Peace" been as tarnished, distorted and desecrated as in Colombia's drug-tainted talks. Under the cover of peace and *"political correctness"*, one of the world's largest terrorist organizations has been ably misleading the country and the world in what clearly characterizes an attempt by TOC to transform Colombia into a full-fledged Narco-state, like its neighbor Venezuela.

The most reprehensible aspect in all of this, though, has been the use of *blackmail* tactics by President Santos who has repeatedly portrayed critics of the talks as *"enemies of peace"* and *"war-mongers."* In line with TOC's distinctive strategies, Santos has monopolized the media, allowed the penetration of Colombia's democratic institutions by elements of organized crime by means of corruption, and fiercely persecuted the country's opposition. Moreover, discernable efforts have been made to reduce the capacities of the country's Armed Forces, perhaps one the most censured and disquieting matters of his highly questionable *"crusade"* for peace.

Nonetheless, the palpable absence of the most rudimentary elements of peace, coupled with FARC's increasing arrogance and unabashed statements, have shown the limits of Santos' *blackmail* tactics both in Colombia and at the international level. Today, more than 75% of the country's citizens oppose the Havana talks and Santos' popularity has hit the rock bottom level of 15%. While many Colombians had *"bought"* the president's idea of peace, the excessive and unreasonable concessions made by the government to the narcoterrorist group since the negotiations began are now perceived as the State's capitulation to terrorism.

"The opposite of Santos' Peace Process isn't war; the opposite is a good peace agreement"

III.   IMPUNITY & VICTIMS

Much like in the case of Fidel Castro in Cuba, the issue of impunity is at the very heart of Colombia's **Peace Talks** with FARC. Most of FARC's 220,000 crimes are classified as crimes against humanity and war crimes. As previously mentioned, the scale and the brutality of the FARC are unparalleled. The narcoterrorist group's crimes, which include massacres, rape, kidnaping, extortion, recruitment of child soldiers and human trafficking, are not only being shoved under the carpet, but Santos also intends to grant FARC's bosses political legitimacy and the ability to run for office. Through an agreement based on

"transitional justice"[32], such crimes would lead to inconsequential deprivation of liberty that would exclude jail time (e.g. house arrest). According to the provisions of the agreement approved by Colombia's Supreme Court, the sole fact of confessing "political" crimes would lead to pardon.

Human Rights Watch condemned the transitional justice deal arguing that it *"sacrificed victims' right to justice"* and that *"sanctions to be used by the tribunal that do not reflect accepted standards of appropriate punishment for grave violations."*

"Under the 'transitional justice' deal it is virtually impossible that Colombia will meet its binding obligations under international law to ensure accountability for crimes against humanity and war crimes."

Human Rights Watch

Amnesty International also expressed its concern in regards to the protection of victims *"Despite the progress towards peace, many seemingly intractable conflict-related human rights and humanitarian challenges persist and could very likely become more acute in a post-conflict environment."* The international human rights organization added, *"For this reason, the groundswell of well-founded optimism should be tempered with caution."*

But most importantly, the **International Criminal Court (ICC)** has also aired its skepticism about the Colombian **Peace Process**. ICC Prosecutor Famous Bensouda said in 2014 *"Intolerance of impunity does not make ICC an enemy of peace."*

"While the ICC may be flexible—in the timing and profile of its investigations and the nature of punishments—we should resist the temptation to confuse flexibility with accepting impunity."

Fatou Bensouda - ICC Prosecutor

---

[32] The United Nations defines **transitional justice** as the full range of processes and mechanisms associated with a society's attempts to come to terms with a legacy of large-scale past abuses, in order to ensure accountability, serve justice and achieve reconciliation.

IV. THE "SANTOS": FIGUREHEADS OF TRANSNATIONAL ORGANIZED CRIME

TOC couldn't have found a better *ambassador* than Colombia's Juan Manuel Santos to do the job. From an aristocratic family, and seemingly part of the establishment, Santos was groomed by Fidel Castro well before he came to power, as a result of his elder brother's close relationship with FARC and with the Cuban leader. Moreover, many believe it is actually Santos' brother, Enrique, who pulls the strings of the whole affair.

Photo: Web

Enrique Santos and Juan Manuel Santos

Dubbed the *"caviar revolutionary"*, upon the fall of communism, Enrique Santos' previous attempts to challenge the State in the 20th century had ended up in utter failure. However, his ties with FARC's chiefs, whom he knew since his youth, remained in force. With the incursion of FARC in the drug trafficking business, Santos the elder saw the opportunity of accomplishing what he had previously failed to achieve, i.e. establishing a *"socialist"* government in Colombia. The Santos brothers are hence part of FARC's transformation from a revolutionary organization into a drug cartel and as such, have *de-facto* become the figureheads of drug trafficking in Colombia and in the region.

Many Colombians claim that President Santos' sole goal is to obtain a Nobel Peace prize, and that might be partly true. Nonetheless, that would be but a welcome spinoff amid a much broader intent. Since coming to power, Santos has closed ranks with *Bolivarian* governments in the region and has kept upsettingly silent about Venezuela's vicious dictatorship. Moreover, despite the incongruity implied in keeping Nicolás Maduro as a *guarantor* of Colombia's peace, the Colombian President has turned a blind eye on the matter.

Accordingly, Santos' *"pacifist"* attitude seems to stem more from a compromise with TOC and the broader *Bolivarian* manifesto, rather than with anything which may closely resemble peace. His efforts to legitimize FARC as a political organization instead of a drug trafficking cartel have been indefatigable, including attempts to make drug trafficking a political crime in order to exonerate FARC members from their criminal involvement in drug trade. The president has gone as far as saying that FARC would be a future partner in the fight against drug trafficking. In my humble view, asking FARC to fight drug trafficking would be like expecting Mother Teresa to train *Daesch* suicide bombers.

Thus far, by the sole fact of sitting more than three years with a terrorist organization in Havana and allowing its superiors to opine freely in respect to the country's internal affairs, Santos has certainly managed to grant the narcoterrorist group an unwarranted degree of legitimacy. Invariably agreeing to all the terms set by FARC in the negotiations, Santos has been stealthily and treacherously putting Colombia in the hands of Transnational Organized Crime.

V.   FOLLOW THE CASH

What many analysts are unsurprisingly concluding is that the real backdrop of the obscure **Peace Talks** is the world's largest ever *money laundering scheme* involving billions of dollars - carefully orchestrated by Transnational Organized Crime (TOC). The latter has infiltrated the entrails of Colombia's public institutions and has also "inevitably" partnered with unscrupulous parties of the country's private sector.

Indeed, one of the darkest grey areas of the unpopular talks is the fate of US $ billions in FARC drug money which neither the drug cartel nor President Santos have publicly accounted for. In fact, FARC has gone as far as saying they have "no knowledge" of the existence of such money – a statement mind-bogglingly backed by Santos who denied the Cartel's involvement in drug trafficking in a visit to the White House in early 2016[33].

Despite FARC's absurd denial, and while it is impossible to know how much the group has in its coffers, a simple multiplication of FARC's alleged US $ 3.4 billion annual profits[34] (which have most likely increased since the beginning of the Havana talks), times the years it has been operating in the drug trafficking business, allows for an estimate of the narcoterrorist group's illicit fortune in the order of tens of billions of dollars.

In order to further illustrate the financial circumstances within which Colombia's **Peace Talks** unfold, in a previous peace attempt by the Colombian government that took place towards the end of the 90's, Colombia's *El Tiempo* informed that New York Stock Exchange (NYSE) President Richard Grasso and NYSE vice presidents Ala Yves Morvan and James Esposito had paid a visit to FARC commanders in the Amazon jungle in 1999. The bizarre invitation had been extended by Colombia's former President Andres Pastrana and aside from vague declarations in regards to its intent, nothing was ever known about the actual content of the meeting. According to Grasso, it had been an interesting exchange of opinions on the global economy and about matters such the

---

[33] According to FARC, the Colombian government treasury should also provide 3% of the country's GDP annually (some US $ 11 billion) for victim reparation.

[34] The Colombian government estimates FARC revenues from drug trafficking at US $ 2.4 to $ 3.5 billion annually.

world's capital markets. Grasso even invited FARC to visit the NYSE in New York. The press was not allowed to cover the meeting.

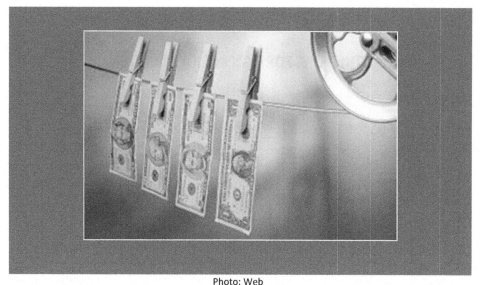

Photo: Web

Money laundering is the vital fluid of transnational organized crime

We are talking big bucks here! And while billions in drug and blood-tainted money seem to be in limbo, billions more have been spent by the Santos government out of the country's treasury in *"persuading"* politicians and the media to support his peace initiative. The outcome: a country whose formerly promising economy is now in dire straits, with rising inflation rates, drastic reductions in exports and a weakening currency. Regrettably, this brings back memories of the first years of Hugo Chávez's Venezuela.

VI.   COLOMBIA'S PEACE IS <u>EVERYBODY'S BUSINESS</u>

The importance of the international framework of Colombia's **Peace Talks** is twofold. Firstly, as previously mentioned, FARC's criminal activities go well beyond Colombia's borders and its links in the ambit of TOC extend its impact around the globe. In this context, it is difficult to comprehend how one country's government alone can negotiate peace with a multinational crime structure. Nonetheless, by portraying the Havana-based talks as a frank and candid pursuit of peace, Santos has also duped the international community and shrewdly obtained its support.

VI.1   YET ANOTHER U.S. FOREIGN POLICY BLUNDER

No questions asked about FARC's billions, President Barack Obama said he would be Santos' *"partner in waging peace"*, and added that he would ask U.S. Congress for US $ 450 million to help Colombia implement its peace deal with the narcoterrorist group. This funding would support, amongst other, de-mining, humanitarian and counter-narcotics activities. The new program, called "Peace Colombia", would represent a 25 percent increase in U.S. funding in relation to 2016 funding levels[35].

In the meantime, U.S.-led assaults against FARC drug operations have waned, Colombia has ended aerial coca field spraying (a cornerstone of drug eradication efforts), and it now heads again the podium of global cocaine producers. Moreover, President Santos intends to request Washington to remove FARC's designation as a Foreign Terrorist Organization (FTO).

The U.S. Administration's announcement in February 2015 of Bernard Aronson as Special Envoy to Colombia's talks was to add to everybody's discomfort. Aronson, former Assistant Secretary of State for Inter-American Affairs, who had been previously involved in peace initiatives in Central America, was known to have significant economic interests at stake in Colombia which largely depended on being in *good terms* with FARC.

According to American journalist and ex-FBI agent Lia Fowler, Aronson is the founder of ACON Investments, an investment firm that holds majority stake in three companies in Colombia, including Vetra Energy, an oil firm acquired in 2013. Vetra operates in areas where FARC conducts intense terrorist activity and was the target of the narcoterrorist group in 2014, when FARC attacks against its facilities resulted in losses of about US $ 8 million. FARC's last attack against Vetra took place in June 2015, just four months after the Aronson's

---

[35] Through the former "Plan Colombia" the US provided US $ 10 billion in funding to Colombia for military and social programs, between 2000 and 2015

appointment. In this last attack, FARC terrorists blocked a Vetra truck convoy and forced the drivers to spill 200,000 gallons of oil, which led to a major environmental disaster. Vetra's President, Humberto Calderon Berti, said at the time that if attacks continued, the company would be obliged to suspend its operations.

According to the U.S. State Department, there is no conflict of interest between Aronson's official duties and his private financial interests. However, what is certain thus far, is that the U.S. Special Envoy has utterly disregarded the disagreement of an ample majority of Colombian people with the talks, as well as warnings issued by several prominent international justice and human rights organizations in regards to the multiple risks these involve. Furthermore, rather than highlighting the incongruity of having Venezuela's Nicolás Maduro, a FARC ally and a vocal U.S. foe, as a guarantor, Aronson has instead opted to travel to Caracas to *"discuss"* Colombia's peace with the Venezuelan president.

Bernard Aronson's main tasks purportedly include, first and foremost, protecting U.S. interests and, amongst these, preserving U.S. extradition policies. Colombia's President Santos, on his side, has said he will do all he can to avoid the extradition of FARC criminals to the U.S. Only time will tell how, and if, Aronson will assert U.S. authority in the realm of international judicial requirements.

The latest foul turn in terms of U.S. involvement in Colombia's Peace was the exclusion of the OAS from the monitoring and supervision of what they have prematurely dubbed the process's *post-conflict* phase. The task was instead assigned to CELAC, the aforementioned multilateral organization founded by Chávez which, as opposed to the OAS, includes Cuba and excludes the US and Canada from its membership.

In the U.S., Republican Senator Marco Rubio warned of the potential for a *"serious and long lasting effect on the national security interest of the United States."* in a letter sent to Aronson on the subject of Colombia's peace initiative. Senator Ileana Ros-Lehtinen, from her side, denounced that Castro had no interest in a genuine peace process, but was rather taking the opportunity to strengthen and legitimize Colombia's FARC. She added that the United States should keep FARC in the list of terrorist organizations and that Colombia's government should not expect U.S. taxpayers to provide additional assistance *"before serious problems are adequately addressed."*

"Members of the FARC have the blood of US citizens on their hands and they should be prosecuted for what the crimes they have committed."

US Senator Ileana Ros-Lehtinen

VI.2   POPE FRANCIS, AGAIN

In view of Popes' Francis known preference for the Latin American *"left"*, few would have been surprised about his support for Colombia's peace negotiations, had it not been for his unpredictable disregard for FARC's 220,000 victims and his implicit support to FARC's impunity. Then again, it does correspond with his indefensible support for Cuba's Castro regime which, as we will see in further detail, is at the very core of Colombia's dubious peace plan. What is more, Latin America's Christians have become one of TOC's main targets and have been repeatedly attacked by FARC.

VI.3   EUROPE OBLIVIOUSNESS

The EU's High Representative, Federica Mogherini, reiterated her confidence in the Havana peace process negotiations and emphasized that *"the EU would be with Colombia all the way"*, by means of a Trust Fund aimed at supporting a *post-conflict* scenario. In the same way both the European Council and the European Parliament offered the Santos government their wholehearted support.

Former Irish Foreign Minister, Eamon Gilmore, was appointed as the High Representative's Special Envoy to the talks, among other things, due to its participation in the Northern Ireland peace process. However, the EU's Special Envoy's past also raised many eyebrows. Gilmore's membership of the radical pro-republican terror and pro-Soviet Official Sinn Fein in the mid-seventies that later became the Workers Party, raised doubts concerning his impartiality.

However, regardless of the EU's representative's evenhandedness, despite the fact that the EU has held extensive discussions about the increasing involvement of TOC in the realm of governance across the world, EU backing to Colombia's drug-tainted talks seems to turn a blind eye on the matter. Mrs. Mogherini seems to ignore their impact on European security particularly in terms of the narcoterrorist group's links with North African Islamic terrorist organizations and the *narco-jihad*.

Note: Upon finalizing this paragraph Ms. Mogherini was shedding tears as a result of two ISIS bombs that had gone off in Brussels's Zaventem Airport and one of its Metro Stations.

VI.4   THE UN'S BYZANTINE VIEWS

The UN has been a *docile* partner of President Santos' Peace Process from the onset. Instead of taking the lead in highlighting the serious pitfalls and risks that the process involves, it has opted for whitewashing FARC's atrocities and granting the narcoterrorist group political legitimacy. This acquiescent stance lies in stark contrast with UN Secretary General Ban Ki Moon's grandiose statements such as, *"Nothing justifies terrorism"* or *"Terrorism is a significant threat to peace"*.

In view of the UN's growing irrelevance and incongruence in the context of today's world affairs, I do not find it worthwhile spending more time on the subject, however, the UN Secretary General might perhaps refer to one of his predecessor's standpoints in regards to the issue of crimes against humanity and war crimes. In 1998, upon discussing Sierra Leone's atrocities, former UN Secretary-General Kofi Annan advised his mediators not to endorse peace agreements that granted amnesty for these categories of crimes. Going a critical step further, it was established ever since that, if national authorities did not apply the full rigor of the law with respect to heinous crimes, the ICC would step in.

VI.5   THE SINISTER TROIKA

As mentioned in Chapter 5, one of the most relevant developments in 21st century Latin America is that alliances between countries have taken the lead over countries' individual stances, and there is no better example of this than Colombia's **Peace Talks**. While the U.S. administration and the EU deal separately with the governments of Cuba, Venezuela and Colombia, they fail to recognize the intimate relationship amongst the three entities, whose common denominator is FARC's drug trafficking enterprise.

According to Colombia's President Santos, the purpose of choosing Cuba for the **Peace Talks** to be held was *"to continue working seriously and with discretion."* Nonetheless, for many analysists, Castro's close links with FARC and his control over Venezuela discernibly undermined the process's neutrality from the outset. Furthermore, President Santos' dubious relationship with the Cuban dictator led to even greater suspicion in regards to the incoherent choice of Cuba as a stage for the talks to take place. As a good friend who teaches International Relations at a local University put it: *"They might as well hold peace talks with the Islamic State in Al-Raqqah"*, the city in Syria where ISIS Headquarters are currently located.

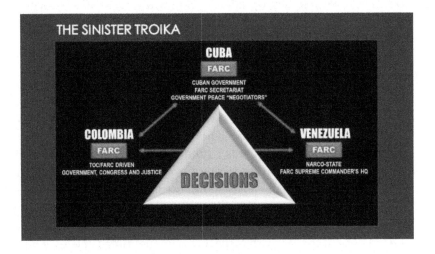

The bottom line is that, today, the fate of Cuba, Venezuela and Colombia's FARC is undivided and, whatever decision is taken in regards to one of these, has direct bearing over the *ensemble*. Meanwhile, the U.S administration, visibly stuck to an outdated piece-meal understanding of Latin Americas' geopolitical dynamics, opens up to Cuba, punishes Venezuela and supports Colombia's **Peace Process** with FARC.

II.   TIME: A KEY FACTOR

In the context of 21st century geopolitics, in which the cadence of events has hastened and leaves no room for choices to linger, time constitutes an ever more important factor of geopolitical decision-making. *"This peace agreement will be a matter of months, not years"*, said Colombia's President Santos upon launching the talks in November 2012, adding that that made his proposal "unique." Four years later, as a result of FARC's delaying tactics, Santos' tender seems to have lost its "uniqueness." In this respect, FARC have repeatedly said that they would take as long as necessary to reach an agreement, sarcastically adding that *"putting strict time limits was not only unrealistic, but it was also a criminal attitude."*

But beyond Santos' inaccuracy, during the years that have elapsed, FARC has been allowed to take bold steps towards its resurgence, structural political changes have transpired and, as previously mentioned, the narcoterrorist group has cynically expanded its criminal enterprise under the cover of "peace." In sum, every day that passes without a proper reaction from the U.S., Europe and the International community *vis-à-vis* Colombia's obscure **Peace Talks**, is a day lost.

VIII.   A GLOOMY OUTLOOK

What most analysts do agree upon is that, regardless of the eventual signing of an agreement with FARC, the structural conditions for the development of illegal activities such as coca cultivation, production and exports will remain in place and other criminal actors will fill the vacuum. Among these actors are the National Liberation Army - ELN[36], the country's second rebel group and FARC's close ally. In addition, other drug trafficking groups such as the terrifying BACRIM[37] criminal gangs, which also enjoy close links with the narcoterrorist organization, are poised to step in.

---

[36] ELN: Ejército de Liberación Nacional
[37] BACRIM: Bandas Criminales

Peace agreements do not necessarily make peace.

I repeat: peace agreements do not necessarily make peace"

Kofi Annan

Previous demobilizations of rebel groups around the world have proven that the sole fact of putting an end to an insurgency does not automatically translate into increased security. While rebel leaders may follow suit, the rank and file will still be tempted by the earnings involved in organized crime leading to the evolution of new criminal structures.

In other words, while information provided by the negotiating table in Havana mentions the successful brokering of partial agreements on issues such as land reform and political participation, the fundamental role of FARC as a member of TOC has been either inadvertently, or purposefully marginalized. However, one thing is certain - this agreement will change the criminal dynamics in Latin America as a whole.

Last but definitely not least, the same as the Islamic Republic of Iran, FARC also firmly embraces its own 50-year-old *"pseudo-sacred"* objective, namely, seizing power. The likeliness that it will capitulate now that it finds itself in a stronger position than ever before is highly questionable.

"Peace is not the absence of war, it is a virtue, a way of thinking,

a disposition for benevolence, confidence and justice"

Baruch Spinoza

CONCLUSIONS

*"The word 'potential' is really important here. In Latin America and the
Caribbean you have weak institutions and very corrupt political vacuums.
It's an easy place for nefarious actors of all stripes to operate."*
Former US Southern Command General John F. Kelly

As happened upon attempting to finalize *El Plan Maestro (The Master Plan)*, concluding an almost self-explanatory matter may turn into a needless and redundant exercise. I will therefore try to highlight a series of facts and prospects that may contribute to this book's main objective: opening America's and Europe's eyes in regards to an impending threat which few have seemingly been able to recognize in its full magnitude and sophistication.

But before we enter the dark matter of fact, allow me to mention, as I did in *El Plan Maestro*, that I am firm believer of the allegory of *The scorpion and the frog*, whereby the intrinsic nature of any living organism is immutable and expecting this nature to change would not only be unnatural, but also highly improbable. In the same vein, the inherent character of the *supreme* aspirations of The Islamic Republic of Iran, Latin America's *"narcopopulism"* and Colombia's FARC's are, in my view, unchangeable and irreversible.

"The object of terrorism is terrorism. The object of oppression is oppression. The object of torture is torture. The object of murder is murder. The object of power is power.

Now do you begin to understand me?"

Eric Arthur Blair, better known as George Orwell

It's a fact that Transnational Organized Crime will continue to thrive and that, unless decisive and commensurate action is taken by the international community, its spread, influence and power will enhance its corrosive potential to impinge on democratic governance and to intensify global crime and international terrorism.

In spite of recent democratic victories in Latin America, as in the case of Argentina, where Cristina Fernández de Kirchner's *Bolivarian*-supported government was voted out of power, there is still a long road ahead in terms of reestablishing the fundamentals of democracy and good governance. On the one hand, the *narcopopulist* outbreak had ample time to take control of the larger part of Latin America. On the other, the fuel on which its engine runs, namely, drug trafficking and corruption, will most likely continue to flow. Of particular importance remain the unusual levels of arms purchases by countries such as Venezuela as well as Russia's and China's growing strategic presence in the U.S. *backyard*.

It is also increasingly clear that Latin America will be unable to avoid the global spread of Islamic extremism and that, sooner or later, it will be the subject of Islamic terror on its territory. Moreover, the lifting of sanctions imposed on the Islamic Republic of Iran will most certainly contribute to the enlargement and tightening of the Islamic nation's grip over the region which will, in turn, augment the possibility of the establishment of nuclear capabilities by governments who share Iran's aversion towards the United States. It is evident that Latin America constitutes the ideal platform for Islamic terror to target the U.S. The issue is no longer a matter of *if*, but rather a matter of *when*, attempts to target U.S. soil will materialize.

"Someday, someone will have to start talking about what will happen to all of us within a decade if we leave the North Koreans and Iranians pursue their nuclear weapons programs"

Lawrence Eagleburger

Evidence that Colombia's President Juan Manuel Santos' pursuit of "peace" is merely the result of an attempt by TOC to spread its influence in the US *backyard* is profuse, and the ripples of the obscure stratagem reach far beyond Colombia's borders and have a direct bearing over the global fight against international terror. Inasmuch as Europe is concerned, as long as FARC and the Latin American drug trafficking industry continue to nurture the emergence of Africa's *narco-jihad*, the EU's anti-terrorist fight will confront a persistent source of terror across the Mediterranean, amid an already destabilizing refuge crisis.

As for U.S. missteps and loss of influence over its own *backyard,* and the current administration's inability to grasp the subtleties of Latin America's 21st century makeover, two steps are urgently required. Firstly, in view of the apparently irreversible character of President Obama's candid policy *vis-à-vis* the Castro regime, remedial action must be taken in the sense of preventing further consolidation of Cuba's vicious control over a growing number of Latin American countries.

Secondly, and perhaps the most urgent step to be taken in order for the first one to transpire, is the **immediate stoppage of Colombia's drug-tainted Peace Talks with FARC** if, as mentioned earlier, both the U.S. and Europe want to prevent the hammering of **the last nail on the coffin** of Latin American democracies, and the ensuing emergence of a terrifying menace which will exceed their response capacity if left unattended. At this stage of the game, and considering that what's at stake as a result of the convoluted account of facts revealed in this book are the lives, safety and future of our children and grandchildren, there's no more room for ambiguity or for gratuitous "political correctness."

Allow me to conclude by making a heartfelt request to those that have taken the time to read my book. The making of both *El Plan Maestro* and *Watch Your Backyard* owes to a genuine concern on my part in regards to the plight of my own family and that of the future generations of the Americas. However, any effort to counter this curse requires the engagement of each and every one of us in the matter. In my view, conveying and expressing our discontent in relation to the way in which events are unfolding in Latin America is not only a vital obligation, it is the unambiguous duty of a true patriot. Hence, my request is simple: **Please watch your backyard!**

"As long as the roots are not severed, all is well.
And all will be well in the garden."

Peter Sellers as Chance the Gardener

Thank you, and God bless you all.

ABOUT THE AUTHOR

Omar Bula Escobar was born in Bogota, Colombia, in 1963. Expert in international geopolitics and sustainable development, the author obtained a Business Administration degree from the European University and the University of Louvain la Neuve, in Belgium, and specialized in Corporate Management and Strategic Negotiation at ADEN/Harvard University. Bula Escobar worked for the United Nations for over 20 years in Europe, the Middle East, Africa and Latin America, and held the post of UN WFP Representative in Dakar, Senegal. The author currently works as an Independent Consultant and as a Lecturer in Management and International Affairs.

BIBLIOGRAPHY AND SOURCES

BY AUTHOR

Abad, Mel. "Russia begins to seal trademark in the Latin America region." Latin Post, 01/29/2016. http://www.latinpost.com/articles/112296/20160129/russia-begins-seal-trademark-latin-america-region.htm

Allen B, West. "Iran is a threat in Latin America." Washington Times, 28/08/2012. http://www.washingtontimes.com/news/2012/aug/28/iran-is-a-threat-in-latin-america/

Allison, Graham. *"The Ultimate Preventable Catastrophe."* C-SPAN Book Discussion on Nuclear Terrorism: The Ultimate Preventable Catastrophe, 19/08/2004. http://www.c-spanvideo.org/program/183099-5

Ángel, Arturo. "Irán, detrás de la presencia de Hezbolá en México, según Wikileaks." 24 Horas, 11/09/2012. http://www.24-horas.mx/iran-detras-de-la-presencia-de-hezbola-en-mexico-segun-wilileaks/

Archbishop Cranmer. "Iran: Hassan Rouhani is neither moderate nor reformist." Archbishop Cranmer, 16/06/2013. http://archbishop-cranmer.blogspot.com/2013/06/iran-hassan-rohani-is-neither-moderate.html

Ávila, Ariel. "¿Por qué negociar con las FARC?" Revista Semana, 27/08/2012.http://www.semana.com/opinion/articulo/por-que-negociar-farc/263703-3

Avni, Benny. "President Obama is the last hope for Latin America's lefty thugs." New York Post, 12/09/2015. http://nypost.com/2015/12/09/president-obama-is-the-last-hope-for-latin-americas-lefty-thugs/

Azevedo, Reinaldo. "Relações Perigosas: As FARC, o PT e o Governo Lula." Veja, Blog, 16/05/2010.http://veja.abril.com.br/blog/reinaldo/geral/relacoes-perigosas-as-farc-o-pt-e-o-governo-lula/

Bárcena, Alicia. "El salto de China en América Latina y el Caribe." El Universal, 05/07/2012. http://www.eluniversal.com/opinion/120705/el-salto-de-china-en-america-latina-y-el-caribe

Beata, Gorka-Winter. "NATO global partnerships in the XXI century" CENAA, 03/26/2016. http://cenaa.org/analysis/nato-global-partnerships-in-the-xxi-century/ Berman, Ilan. "Iran Courts Latin America." Middle East Forum, summer 2012. http://www.meforum.org/3297/iran-latin-america

Bethancourt, Grisel. "Globalización y Narcotráfico." Panamá América, 10/06/2000. http://www.panamaamerica.com.pa/notas/272798-globalizacion-y-narcotrafico

Boniface, Dexter y Azpuru Dinorah. "U.S.-Latin America Relations in the Post-Chávez Era." Fletcher Forum, 26/03/2013. http://www.fletcherforum.org/2013/03/26/boniface_azpuru/

Bolilan, Nens. "President Obama avoids pressing issues in Latin America in State of the Union address." Latin One, 03/25/2016. http://www.latinone.com/articles/30683/20160114/president-obama-avoids-pressing-issues-latin-america-state-union-address.htm

Botta, Paulo. "Irán en América Latina: Desde Venezuela hacia Brasil." CEMOC, último acceso 03/07/2013. http://www.cemoc.com.ar/IranenAmericaLatina.pdf

Brewer, Jerry. "Terrorism Roots in the Tri-border Area of South America." MexiData, 02/01/2010. http://mexidata.info/id2539.html

Buckley, Ed. "International groups skeptical of Colombia peace process." The City Paper, Bogotá, 02/11/2016. http://thecitypaperbogota.com/news/international-groups-skeptical-of-colombia-peace-process/11796

Bueso, Alexander. "Iran and Venezuela accused of financing Spain's Podemos by alleged DEA informant." Yahoo Finance, 01/14/2016. https://uk.finance.yahoo.com/news/iran-venezuela-accused-financing-spains-150200740.html

Bula Escobar, Omar. "El Plan Maestro: Irán, el ALBA, FARC y el Terror Nuclear." Amazon & Kindle Books. September, 2013. http://el-planmaestro.blogspot.com.co/

Burcher Uribe, Catalina. "Organized crime, Colombia's peace spoiler?" Open Security, 08/27/2014. https://www.opendemocracy.net/opensecurity/catalina-uribe-burcher/organized-crime-colombia's-peace-spoiler

Cancel, Daniel. "Venezuela to Develop Nuclear Energy with Russian Help (Update1)." Bloomberg.com, 13/09/2009. http://www.bloomberg.com/apps/news?pid=newsarchive&sid=aEIQ3UEU9eYM

Carnes, Harley. "What If: The Greatest Threat - An Al Qaida-Drug Cartel Alliance." Fox News, 22/01/2012. http://latino.foxnews.com/latino/news/2012/01/22/what-if-greatest-threat-al-qaida-drug-cartel-alliance/

Caroll, JP. "SOTU: President ignores socialist and communist aggression in Latin America. Daily Caller, 01/13/2016.

http://dailycaller.com/2016/01/13/sotu-president-ignores-socialist-and-communist-aggression-in-latin-america/#ixzz41Qd0BaeF

Century, Douglas. "ISIS and the new face of narcoterrorism." Tablet, 10/06/2014. http://www.tabletmag.com/scroll/186110/isis-and-the-new-face-of-narcoterrorism

Chaya, George. "Avance islamista en América Latina." OLADD, 12/09/2008. http://oladd.com/bin/content.cgi?news=528

Chirinos, Carlos. "Rusia regresa 'para quedarse'." BBC Mundo, 10/11/2008.http://news.bbc.co.uk/hi/spanish/latin_america/newsid_7720000/7720403.stm

Cooper, Hank. "A Cuban Missile Crisis for Today?" National Review, 22/10/2012. http://www.nationalreview.com/articles/331114/cuban-missile-crisis-today-hank-cooper

Corzo, Pedro. "El uranio ecuatoriano en la mira de Irán." Interamerican Security Watch (IASW), 18/01/2012. http://interamericansecuritywatch.com/el-uranio-ecuatoriano-en-la-mira-de-iran/

Corzo, Pedro. "El fundamentalismo islámico en América Latina." Analítica, 13/01/2012. http://www.analitica.com/va/internacionales/opinion/5097046.asp

Daremblum, Jaime. "Al Qaeda in Brazil?" Eurasia Review – Hudson Institute, 08/04/2011. http://www.eurasiareview.com/08042011-al-qaeda-in-brazil-oped/

Das, Achintya. "The Growing Influence of Jihad in Latin America." International Unity for Equality, 20/04/2013. http://www.iufe.org/2013/04/the-growing-influence-of-jihad-in-latin.html

De la Cruz, Alberto. "Obama should support democracy in Latin America, not embrace tyranny and repression." Babalu Blog, 01/16/2016. http://babalublog.com/2016/01/16/obama-should-support-democracy-in-latin-america-not-embrace-tyranny-and-repression/

Delgado Kling, Paula. "FARC manuals instruct cruelty in treating hostages." Talking About Colombia, 28/02/2012. http://talkingaboutcolombia.com/2012/02/28/farc-manuals-instruct-cruelty-in-treating-hostages/

Diehl, Sarah. "Venezuela's Search for Nuclear Power - or Nuclear Prestige." Nuclear Threat Initiative (NTI), 07/05/2009. http://www.nti.org/analysis/articles/venezuelas-search-nuclear-power/

Deustua, Alejandro. "El terrorismo y el narcotráfico de alcance global." Contexto, 25/07/2005. http://www.contexto.org/docs/2005/edit188.html

Dinatale, Martin. "Inauguran en Quito la nueva y moderna sede de la UNASUR, que se llamará Néstor Kirchner." La Nación, 12/02/2014.
http://www.lanacion.com.ar/1748690-inauguran-en-quito-la-nueva-y-moderna-sede-de-la-unasur-que-se-llamara-nestor-kirchner

Dvorak, Kimberly. "Afghan Heroin and Mexican cartels are a recipe for disaster." Kimberly Dvorak, 01/06/2011.
http://kimberlydvorak.blogspot.com/2011/06/afghan-heroin-and-mexican-cartels-are.html

Encarnaci, Omar. "The Costs of Indifference: Latin America and the Bush Era." Centre for World Dialogue, 2008.
http://www.worlddialogue.org/content.php?id=432

Escurra, Marta. "Paraguayan guerrillas were trained by the FARC." Infosur, 16/03/2010.
http://infosurhoy.com/cocoon/saii/xhtml/en_GB/features/saii/features/main/2010/03/16/feature-01

Espinoza, Andrea. "La industria del narcotráfico se expande en Ecuador," El País, Internacional, 31/05/2012.
http://internacional.elpais.com/internacional/2012/05/31/actualidad/1338450249_507702.html

Fara, Douglas. "Denuncian la cooperación nuclear entre Argentina e Irán." Informador Público, 12/02/2013. http://site.informadorpublico.com/?p=26039

Farah, Joseph. "Islam on march south of border." WND, 06/07/2005.
http://www.wnd.com/2005/06/30674/

Farrar Wellman, Ariel. "Bolivia-Iran foreign relations." Iran Tracker, 08/04/2010. http://www.irantracker.org/foreign-relations/bolivia-iran-foreign-relations

Fleischman, Luis. "Iran's expansive role in the Middle East and Latin America, and the nuclear negotiations." Center for Security Policy, 02/26/2015. http://www.centerforsecuritypolicy.org/2015/02/26/irans-expansive-role-in-the-middle-east-and-latin-america-and-the-nuclear-negotiations/

Flibbert, Andrew. "The Art of the 'Impossible': Writing Peace Agreements during War." Trinity College and New York University, October 2003. http://www.apsanet.org/imgtest/PSOct03Flibbert.pdf

Forero, Juan. "South American Leaders Assail U.S. Access to Colombian Military Bases." The Washington Post, 29/08/2009. http://www.washingtonpost.com/wp-dyn/content/article/2009/08/28/AR2009082803768.html

Fox Share, Edward. "Illegal Mining Colombia's Biggest Challenge: Police Chief." Ministry of Natural Resources and the Environment, XXXX, 20/04/2012. http://www.nre.gov.gy/Illegal%20Mining%20Colombia's%20Biggest%20Challenge.%20April%2024%202012.html

Fowler, Lia. "Bernard Aronson y sus intereses económicos en Colombia." Debate, 03/15/2016. http://periodicodebate.com/index.php/welcome/item/11133-cnews-2016-03-14-2

Franks, Jeff . "Iranian leader says Cuba, Iran think alike." Reuters, 01/12/2012.http://www.reuters.com/article/2012/01/12/us-cuba-iran-idUSTRE80B1KC20120112

Fuentes Chavarriga, Julio. "Venezuela se arma...." Biblioteca del Congreso Nacional de Chile, 17/07/2010. http://www.ligasmayores.bcn.cl/content/view/887179/Venezuela-se-arma.html

Gallucci, Maria. "Lifting US Sanctions on Cuba Has Economic Perks But Isn't A Boon For Trade, Analysts Say." International Business Times, 12/17/2014. http://www.ibtimes.com/lifting-us-sanctions-cuba-has-economic-perks-isnt-boon-trade-analysts-say-1761780

García, Carlos. "Armamentismo en América Latina: más allá de Chávez." Revista Semana, 07/04/2010. http://www.semana.com/mundo/america-latina/articulo/armamentismo-america-latina-mas-alla-chavez/115248-3

Gato, Pablo y Windrem, Robert. "Hezbollah builds a Western base." NBC News, 05/09/2007. http://www.nbcnews.com/id/17874369/ns/world_news-americas/t/hezbollah-builds-western-base/#.UXMUNaI3u8A

Gerami, Nima. "Venezuela: Un Perfil Nuclear." Carnegie Endowment for International Peace, 18/12/2008. http://npsglobal.org/esp/titulares/13-noticias/424-venezuela-un-perfil-nuclear-nima-gerami-y-sharon-squassoni.html

Ghitis, Frida. "Can Obama get Latin America right?" CNN, 04/11/2015. http://edition.cnn.com/2015/04/10/opinions/ghitis-obama-summit-americas/

Gil, Chema. "Colombia: Los Narcoterroristas de las FARC ya han ganado frente al Gobierno." Globedia, 30/12/2012. http://co.globedia.com/colombia-narcoterroristas-farc-ganado-frente-Gobierno

Glenny, Misha. "Misha Glenny investigates global crime networks." Ted Talks, 09/14/2009. https://www.youtube.com/watch?v=XO1Me-MY-Q0

Glenny, Misha. "The war on drugs has failed." Global Initiative, 02/25/2016. http://www.globalinitiative.net/its-time-to-tell-the-emperor-the-war-on-drugs-has-failed/

Gómez, Camel. "¿Que puede ofrecer el Islam en América Latina?" IslamOrient.com, último acceso 03/07/2013. http://www.islamoriente.com/sites/default/files/cckfilefield/Article_pdf_file/Qu%C3%A9%20puede%20ofrecer%20el%20Islam%20en%20Am%C3%A9rica%20Latina.pdf

Guillén, Gonzalo. "Revelan Nexos de Raúl Castro con el Narcotráfico." La Cuba Hispana, último acceso 02/07/2013. http://www.lacubahispana.net/documentos/Portada/La%20financiaci%C3%B3 n%20del%20mal.htm

Guzmán, Jorge. "Bolivia anuncia programa atómico." Voz de las Américas, 02/06/2011. http://www.voanoticias.com/content/america-latina-bolivia-relaciones-iran-energia-atomica-prohttp://seccionsegunda.blogspot.com/2011/06/inaugurada-en-bolivia-escuela-de.html

Henderson, "Iran's Mahmoud Ahmadinejad and Venezuela's Hugo Chavez taunt US over 'big atomic bomb'." The Telegraph, 10/01/2012. http://www.telegraph.co.uk/news/worldnews/middleeast/iran/9005134/Irans -Mahmoud-Ahmadinejad-and-Venezuelas-Hugo-Chavez-taunt-US-over-big-atomic-bomb.html

Holmberg, Jhon. "Narcoterrorism." 05/11/2009. http://traccc.gmu.edu/pdfs/student_research/HolmbergNarcoterrorism.pdf

Horsley, Scott. "With A Handshake and More, Obama Shifts U.S.-Latin America Policy." NPR, 04/13/2015. http://www.npr.org/sections/itsallpolitics/2015/04/13/399236626/with-a-handshake-and-more-obama-shifts-u-s-latin-america-policy

Ileana Ros-Lehtinen. "En reunión con el Presidente Santos, Ros-Lehtinen expresó oposición por negociaciones con las FARC." Ileana Ros Lehtinen, 02/03/2016. https://ros-lehtinen.house.gov/press-release/en-reuni%C3%B3n-con-el-presidente-santos-ros-lehtinen-expres%C3%B3-oposici%C3%B3n-por-negociaciones

Insulza, José Miguel. "Las drogas y el debilitamiento del Estado / Análisis." El Tiempo, Política, 17/05/2013. http://www.eltiempo.com/politica/anlisis-sobre-el-tema-de-las-drogas-por-jos-miguel-insulza_12807065-4

Iturra Alonso, María T. "Narcotráfico Una Industria Global." Buenas Tareas, julio 2011. http://www.buenastareas.com/ensayos/Narcotrafico-Una-Industria-Global/2530246.html

Jamasmie, Cecilia. "Latin America poised to become uranium superpower." Mining.com, 09/29/2012.
http://www.mining.com/latin-american-posed-to-be-a-uranium-superpower-10604/

Jackson, David. "Obama: Nuclear terrorism is 'the single biggest threat' to U.S." USA Today, 11/04/2010.
http://content.usatoday.com/communities/theoval/post/2010/04/obama-kicks-off-nuclear-summit-with-five-leader-meetings/1#.Uakp8dl3u8A

James, Ian. "Obama victory a relief for Latin American left." Associated Press, 07/11/2012. http://news.yahoo.com/obama-victory-relief-latin-american-left-210547152.html

Jiménez Pereira, Alfredo. "América Latina continúa carrera armamentista." Los Tiempos, 20/08/2012.
http://www.lostiempos.com/diario/actualidad/internacional/20120820/america-latina-continua-en-carrera-armamentista_182642_386762.html

Justo, Marcelo. "China y América Latina, ¿una relación con futuro?" BBC Mundo, 22/10/2012.
http://www.bbc.co.uk/mundo/noticias/2012/10/121017_china_comercio_america_latina_ar.shtml

Kahlili, Reza. "Opinion: Iran is Building a Secret Missile Installation in Venezuela." Fox News Latino, 17/05/2011.
http://latino.foxnews.com/latino/news/2011/05/17/iran-building-secret-missile-installation-venezuela/#ixzz2PisDbWCX

Kaplan, Michael. "ISIS radioactive 'dirty bomb'? ISLAMIC STATE group sought nuclear material in Belgium, authorities say." International Business Times, 02/29/2016. http://www.ibtimes.com/isis-radioactive-dirty-bomb-islamic-state-group-sought-nuclear-material-belgium-2327333?mkt_tok=3RkMMJWWfF9wsRovvaTJZKXonjHpfsX57eokXqG%2FlMI%2FOER3fOvrPUfGjl4ISMdrI%2BSLDwEYGJlv6SgFSrnAMbBwzLgFWhI%3D

Karmon, Ely Dr. "Hezbollah America Latina: Strange Group or Real Threat [Long, potentially ominous]." Free Republic, 14/11/2006. http://www.freerepublic.com/focus/f-news/1773483/posts

Kasperowicz, Pete. "Ros-Lehtinen warns against Iran's interest in Ecuador's uranium." The Hill, 01/12/2012. http://thehill.com/blogs/floor-action/house/203805-ros-lehtinen-warns-against-irans-interest-in-ecuadors-uranium

Keating, Joshua. "How worried should we be about Farqaueda." Foreign Policy, 05/01/2010. http://blog.foreignpolicy.com/posts/2010/01/05/how_worried_should_we_be_about_farqaeda

Khalili, Reza. "Iran fans out 40,000 agents in South America." The Clarion Project, 07/15/2012. http://www.clarionproject.org/analysis/iran-fans-out-40000-agents-south-america

Kouri, Jim. "Al-Qaeda and FARC: The Unholy Alliance." Canada Free Press, 27/06/2010. http://www.canadafreepress.com/index.php/article/24739

Kredo, Adam. "The Iran, Hezbollah, Venezuela Axis." Free Beacon, 22/03/2013. http://freebeacon.com/the-iran-hezbollah-venezuela-axis/

Langlois, Jill. "FARC makes up to $3.5 billion from drug trade." The Global Post, 25/10/2012. http://www.globalpost.com/dispatch/news/regions/americas/colombia/121025/farc-makes-35-billion-drug-trade

Lake, Eli. "Alarm Grows in Congress, U.S. Intelligence Over Iran's Latin America Threat," The Daily Beast, 15/12/2011. http://www.thedailybeast.com/articles/2011/12/15/alarm-grows-in-congress-u-s-intelligence-over-iran-s-latin-america-threat.html

Lamothe, Dan. "Islamic State could infiltrate U.S. through Caribbean and South America, general says." Washington Post, 03/12/2015. https://www.washingtonpost.com/news/checkpoint/wp/2015/03/12/islamic-state-could-infiltrate-united-states-through-caribbean-general-says/

Lautenschlager, Daniel. "Uranium mining: just another Venezuela-Iran connection." The Americas Report, 11/18/2011.

http://www.theamericasreport.com/2011/11/18/uranium-mining-just-another-venezuela-iran-connection/

León, Juanita. "La fuerza militar con la que llegan las FARC a la mesa." La Silla Vacía, 12/11/2012. http://lasillavacia.com/historia/la-fuerza-militar-con-la-que-llegan-las-farc-la-mesa-37103

Lopez, Linette. "It's time to start worrying about what Russia's been up to in Latin America." Business Insider, 03/27/2015. http://www.businessinsider.com/its-time-to-start-worrying-about-what-russias-been-up-to-in-latin-america-2015-3

López Zea, Leopoldo y Zea Prado, Irene. "Los Tres Pilares de Rusia en América Latina." Revistas UNAM, último acceso 02/07/2013. http://www.revistas.unam.mx/index.php/rri/article/view/21562

Lorenz, J. Haas, "Iran´s Threat in America's Backyard." International Business Times, 01/11/2012. http://www.ibtimes.com/irans-threat-americas-backyard-857505#

Machado, Carlos. "Fundamentalismo Islámico en América Latina." Periódico Tribuna, 02/11/2007. http://periodicotribuna.com.ar/3302-fundamentalismo-islamico-en-america-latina.html

Mahjar-Barducci, Anna. "Iran helping Bolivia Build Nuclear Power Plant." Gatestone Institute, 03/12/2010.
http://www.gatestoneinstitute.org/1692/bolivia-iran

Marcella, Gabriel. "China's Military Activity in Latin America." America's Quarterly, last access 03/07/2013.
http://www.americasquarterly.org/Marcella

Marquis, Christopher. "Latin American Allies of U.S.: Docile and Reliable No Longer." New York Times, 09/01/2004.
http://www.nytimes.com/2004/01/09/politics/09SUMM.html

Massé, Frederick. "Irán, América Latina y Colombia." Ministerio de Relaciones Exteriores, Colombia. Ultimo acceso 03/07/2013.
http://www.cancilleria.gov.co/sites/default/files/Iran,%20Am%C3%A9rica%20l atina%20y%20Colombia%20-
%20Fr%C3%A9d%C3%A9ric%20Mass%C3%A9_0.pdf

McDermott, Jeremy. "Posibles Escenarios de una Fragmentación o Criminalización de las FARC." Insight Crime Analysis, 20/05/2013.
http://es.insightcrime.org/paz-farc/las-farc-2-los-escenarios-de-una-posible-fragmentacion-o-criminalizacion-de-las-farc

McDermott, Jeremy. "Bolivia: The new hub for drug trafficking in South America." Insight Crime, 10/16/2014.
http://www.insightcrime.org/investigations/bolivia-the-new-hub-for-drug-trafficking-in-south-america

Margolis, Mack. "Bolivia's hollow victory in the war on drugs." Bloomberg, 08/24/2015.
http://www.bloombergview.com/articles/2015-08-24/bolivia-s-hollow-victory-in-the-war-on-drugs

Meacham, Carl. "U.S. needs new thinking for Latin American policy." Miami Herald, 20/03/2013. http://www.miamiherald.com/2013/03/20/3297243/us-needs-new-thinking-for-latin.html

Meacham, Carl. "Is Russia moving in on Latin America?" Center for Strategic and International Studies, 03/25/2014. httsis.org/publication/russia-moving-latin-america

Mergier, Anne Marie. "Jihadists and Latin American drug traffickers merge – Africa Connection." Borderland Beat, 02/15/2013. http://www.borderlandbeat.com/2013/02/jihadists-and-latin-american-drug.html

Mesa-Lago, Carmelo. "La relación económica de Cuba con Venezuela: Situación actual y perspectivas." Convivencia Cuba, último acceso 03/07/2013. http://www.convivenciacuba.es/index.php/economa-mainmenu-56/841-la-relacin-econmica-de-cuba-con-venezuela-situacin-actual-y-perspectivas

Mezzofiore, Gianluca. "Air Cocaine: Al-Qaeda ally with Colombia's drug cartels to smuggle drugs into Europe." International Business Times, 11/30/2014. http://www.ibtimes.co.uk/air-cocaine-al-qaeda-ally-colombias-drug-cartels-smuggle-drugs-into-europe-1477338

Miroff, Nick. "Cuba: Colombia's peacemaker?" The Global Post, 19/11/2012. http://www.globalpost.com/dispatch/news/regions/americas/cuba/121119/colombia-farc-ceasefire-peace-talks-havana-role-negotiations

Monda, David. "Peace Can't Be Built on Impunity." New York Times, 23/03/2012. http://www.nytimes.com/2012/03/24/opinion/peace-cant-be-built-on-impunity.html?_r=0

Morrison, David. "Hugo Chavez: The man who raised oil prices." David Morrison, last access 03/07/2013. http://www.david-morrison.org.uk/venezuela/chavez.htm

Morss, Elliot. "Ecuador: Effects of global recession and future prospects." Morss Global Finance, 03/12/2010. http://www.morssglobalfinance.com/ecuador-effects-of-global-recession-and-future-prospects/

Mosendz, Polly. "President Obama calls for lifting Cuban embargo in State Of The Union address." NEWSWEEK, 12/01/2016. http://www.newsweek.com/cuba-embargo-president-obama-state-union-414972

Morgenthau, Robert. "The Link between Iran and Venezuela A Crisis in the Making?" Latin American Herald Tribune, 07/01/2013. http://laht.com/article.asp?ArticleId=343289&CategoryId=10718

Moura, Felipe. "Conheça o Foro de São Paulo, o maior inimigo do Brasil." Veja, 03/24/2014. http://veja.abril.com.br/blog/felipe-moura-brasil/america-latina/conheca-o-foro-de-sao-paulo-o-maior-inimigo-do-brasil/

Muggah, Robert y McDermott, Jeremy. "A Massive Drug Trade, and No Violence." The Atlantic, 24/04/2013. http://www.theatlantic.com/international/archive/2013/04/a-massive-drug-trade-and-no-violence/275258/

Murphy, Helen. "FARC controls 60 percent of drug trade - Colombia's police chief." Reuters, 22/04/2013. http://uk.reuters.com/article/2013/04/22/uk-colombia-rebels-police-idUKBRE93L18Y20130422

Naím, Moisés. "La cara oscura de la globalización." El País, 14/01/2007. http://elpais.com/diario/2007/01/14/negocio/1168784069_850215.html

Naím, Moisés. "Mafia States." Foreign Affairs, Op-Ed, 25/04/2012. http://carnegieendowment.org/2012/04/25/mafia-states/ah37

Nagraj, Neil. "Colombian FARC rebels, al-Qaeda joining forces to smuggle cocaine into Europe, says DEA." Daily News, 05/01/2010. http://www.nydailynews.com/news/world/colombian-farc-rebels-al-qaeda-joining-forces-smuggle-cocaine-europe-dea-article-1.460181#ixzz2Sej6J900

Neumann, Vanessa. "The New Nexus of Narcoterrorism: Hezbollah and Venezuela." Foreign Policy Research Institute, last access 03/07/2013. http://www.fpri.org/enotes/2011/201112.neumann.narcoterrorism.html

Neumann, Vanessa. "The Middle Eastern-Latin American terrorist connection." Foreign Policy Research Institute, May 2011. http://www.fpri.org/docs/media/201105.neumann.latinamericanterrorist.pdf

Noriega, Roger y Cárdenas José. "La creciente amenaza de Hezbollah en América Latina." American Enterprise Institute for Public Policy Research (AEI), October 2011. http://www.aei.org/files/2011/10/17/2011-03%20Spanish%20LAO.pdf

O'Brien, Matt. "Venezuela is on the brink of a complete economic collapse." Washington Post, 01/29/2006. https://www.washingtonpost.com/news/wonk/wp/2016/01/29/venezuela-is-on-the-brink-of-a-complete-collapse/

O 'Grady, Mary Anastasia. "Opinión: El eje de la cocaína Bolivia-yihad." Wall Street Journal, 02/08/2016.
http://lat.wsj.com/articles/SB11367896514743233719004581527281387768392?tesla=y

O 'Grady, Mary Anastasia. "Opinión: Los demócratas de Cuba necesitan el apoyo de EE.UU." Wall Street Journal, 01/25/2016.
http://lat.wsj.com/articles/SB10594439783712603933404581498973619343428?tesla=y

Olander, Eric. "China's presence in South America is considerably larger than in Africa, but we never hear about it." Huffington Post, 02/22/2016.
http://www.huffingtonpost.com/eric-olander/china-south-america-china-africa_b_9274096.html

O'Neill, Claire. "Alleged FARC Scheme Swapped Cocaine for West African Arms." Insight Crime Analysis, 12/04/2013.
http://www.insightcrime.org/news-briefs/farc-cocaine-arms-west-africa-guinea-bissau

Ortiz, Román. "Carrera Armamentista en América Latina: armas, armas, armas." Infolatam, 06/09/2009. http://www.infolatam.com/2009/09/07/carrera-armamentista-en-america-latina-armas-armas-armas/

O'Toole, Kathleen. "Why peace Agreements often fail to end civil wars." Stanford News Service, 19/11/1997. http://news.stanford.edu/pr/97/971119civilwar.html

Pachico, Elyssa. "Panama FARC Camps Highlight Need for Joint Security Work with Colombia." Interamerican Security Watch, 30/03/2012. http://interamericansecuritywatch.com/panama-farc-camps-highlight-need-for-joint-security-work-with-colombia/

Pardo, Rodrigo. "Latin America without Chavez." Project Syndicate, 05/04/2013. http://www.project-syndicate.org/commentary/post-ch-vez-venezuela-and-latin-american-diplomacy-by-rodrigo-pardo

Paullier, Juan. "¿Carrera Armamentista sudamericana?" BBC Mundo, 10/08/2009. http://www.bbc.co.uk/mundo/america_latina/2009/08/090807_carrerarmamentista_sudamerica_jp.shtml

Pérez Molina, Otto. "We have to find new solutions to Latin America's drugs nightmare." The Guardian, 07/04/2012. http://www.guardian.co.uk/commentisfree/2012/apr/07/latin-america-drugs-nightmare

Pickrell, John. "Introduction: The Nuclear Age." New Scientist, 04/09/2006. http://www.newscientist.com/article/dn9956-instant-expert-the-nuclear-age.html

Pineda, Saúl. "Organized crime and narcotics." Colombian Council on International Relations. http://www.consejomexicano.org/Emails/PaperPineda.pdf

Pessin, Al. "NATO Seeks to Redefine Role, Again." Voice of America News, 10/06/2010. http://www.voanews.com/content/nato-seeks-to-redefine-role-again-96185914/119378.html

Powell, Stewart M. "Iran's ties to Latin America worry U.S." San Francisco Chronicle, 11/08/2012. http://www.sfgate.com/world/article/Iran-s-ties-to-Latin-America-worry-U-S-3781854.php#ixzz2Pi1Hpp2P

Rathbone, John Paul. "The 'Great Game' of Colombia's peace process." Financial Times, Blogs, 05/09/2012. http://blogs.ft.com/the-world/2012/09/the-great-game-of-colombias-peace-process/#axzz2AVHWtTZr

Realuyo, Celina. "The Terror-Crime Nexus." The Cypher Brief, 12/01/2015. https://www.thecipherbrief.com/article/terror-crime-nexus

Rebossio, Alejandro. "Argentina e Irán reanudan el diálogo después de seis años de tensión." El País, Internacional, 29/09/2102. http://internacional.elpais.com/internacional/2012/09/29/actualidad/134887 2324_572938.html

Reyes, Gerardo. "Las FARC, los terroristas más peligrosos de América." El Nuevo Herald, Latin American Studies, 13/10/2001. http://www.latinamericanstudies.org/farc/farc-peligrosos.htm

Rico, Maite. "Las FARC hallan refugio en Ecuador." El País, Internacional, 12/03/2008. http://elpais.com/diario/2008/03/12/internacional/1205276401_850215.html

Riding, Alan. "NATO Struggling to Redefine Itself." New York Times, 24/09/1990. http://www.nytimes.com/1990/09/24/world/nato-struggling-to-redefine-itself.html

Riera Casany, Joan Manuel. "¿El narcotráfico futuro rector de la economía mundial?" Las Drogas. Info, septiembre 2009. http://www.lasdrogas.info/opiniones/281

Riera Casany, Joan Manuel. "El narcotráfico y la globalización." Instituto para el Estudio de Adicciones (IEA), marzo 2008. http://www.ieanet.com/opiniones/252

Robinson, Nina. "The Impact of drug trafficking and organized crime in Colombia." Control Risk, last access 13/07/2013. http://www.controlrisks.com/webcasts/studio/foco/foco_issue_1/english/article_2.html

Roque, Juan Carlos. "El Islam en América Latina." Radio Nederland (RNW), 29/08/2005. http://www.rnw.nl/espanol/article/el-islam-en-america-latina

Rollins, John and Sun Wyler, Liana. "Terrorism and Transnational Crime: Foreign Policy for Congress." Congressional Research Service, 06/11/2013. https://www.fas.org/sgp/crs/terror/R41004.pdf

Romero, Maria Teresa. "Terrorism Leaves No Room for Latin America to Sit on the Sidelines." Panam Post, 11/23/2015. https://panampost.com/maria-teresa-romero/2015/11/23/terrorism-leaves-no-room-for-latin-america-to-sit-on-the-sidelines/

Rubin, Michael. "Hezbollah Raises Latin American Profile." Commentary Magazine, 09/15/2012. http://www.commentarymagazine.com/2012/09/15/hezbollah-raises-latin-american-profile/

Santorum, Rick. "Jihadist Training Camps In South America' In Arguing For Border Crackdown." The Huffington Post, 04/02/2011. http://www.huffingtonpost.com/2011/02/04/rick-santorum-border-jihadist-training-camps_n_818623.html

Salazar, Marianella. "Un patio trasero con Uranio." El Nacional, 03/18/2015. http://www.el-nacional.com/marianella_salazar/patio-trasero-uranio_0_593340841.html#.VQnLDvcGNb5.twitter

Sanchez, Alejandro. "Geopolitical considerations of the NATO-Colombia cooperation agreement." E-International Relations, 02/28/2014. http://www.e-ir.info/2014/02/28/geopolitical-considerations-of-the-nato-colombia-cooperation-agreement/

Sanderson, Thomas. "Transnational Terror and Organized Crime: Blurring the Lines." Project Muse, winter-spring 2004. http://www.shirleymohr.com/JHU/Sample_Articles_JHUP/SAI_2004_24_1.pdf

Santos, Juan Manuel. "Alocución del Presidente de la República, Juan Manuel Santos sobre el 'Acuerdo General para la Terminación del Conflicto'." Presidencia de la República de Colombia, 04/09/2012. http://wsp.presidencia.gov.co/Prensa/2012/Septiembre/Paginas/20120904_0 1.aspx

Saturday, Helene. "FARC SICÓPATA Y GENOCIDA." Juzgar a Chávez, 15/10/2011.
http://www.juzgarachavez.org/index.php?option=com_content&view=article &id=285:farc-sicopata-y-genocida-masacre-de-san-salvadorvideo-imagenes-fuertes&catid=73:videos&Itemid=79

Schvindlerman, Julián. "Denuncian pacto nuclear Argentina-Venezuela-Irán." Infobae, 24/11/2011. http://america.infobae.com/notas/38705-La-Argentina-y-el-programa-nuclear-de-Iran

Schvindlerman, Julián. "La Argentina y el programa nuclear de Irán." Infobae, 24/11/2011.http://america.infobae.com/notas/38705-La-Argentina-y-el-programa-nuclear-de-Iran

Seils, Paul. "Intolerance of impunity does not make ICC an enemy of peace." Open Democracy, 19/18/2014. https://www.opendemocracy.net/openglobalrights/paul-seils/intolerance-of-impunity-does-not-make-icc-enemy-of-peace

Ser, Sam. "Lieberman claims Venezuela helps fund Iran's nuclear program." Times of Israel, 27/06/2012. http://www.timesofisrael.com/liberman-claims-venezuela-helps-fund-irans-nuclear-program/

Shinkman, Paul. "Military fears ISIS is eyeing drug-smuggling routes to enter U.S." US News, 04/29/2015. http://www.usnews.com/news/articles/2015/04/29/military-fears-isis-is-eyeing-drug-smuggling-routes-to-enter-us

Smink, Verónica. "Qué gana Irán con el acuerdo con Argentina sobre la AMIA." BBC Mundo, 28/02/2013. http://www.bbc.co.uk/mundo/noticias/2013/02/130226_amia_que_gana_iran_vs.shtml

Smith, Tonny. "Raúl Castro - Fidel Castro -CUBA NARCOTRAFICO Pablo Escobar." YouTube, 17/10/2012. http://www.youtube.com/watch?v=kzCiD1xfuBM

Soibel, Leah y Gorodzinsky, Aaron. "La reciente influencia política, militar y económica de Irán en América Latina." The Israel Project, último acceso 03/07/2013. http://www.theisraelproject.org/site/apps/nlnet/content2.aspx?c=ewJXKcOUJ llaG&b=7840705&ct=11150229#.UXw_sKI3u8A

Squassoni, Sharon. "Nuclear: Latin American Revival." Carnegie Endowment for International Peace, 17/02/2009. http://carnegieendowment.org/2009/02/17/nuclear-latin-american-revival/y0h

Spinetto, Juan Pablo. "China grows its South America influence after commodity bust." Bloomberg, 05/19/2015. http://www.bloomberg.com/news/articles/2015-05-19/china-grows-south-america-sway-as-commodity-bust-cheapens-assets

Stakelbeck, Eric. "Iran, Hezbollah Tentacles Reaching Latin America." CBN News, 12/12/2011. http://www.cbn.com/cbnnews/world/2011/december/iran-hezbollah-spread-tentacles-to-latin-america/

Stedman, Stephen. "Reflections on Implementing Peace Agreements in Civil Wars." Center for International Security and Cooperation at Stanford University, summer 2001. http://www.glencree.ie/site/documents/publications_stedman_paper.pdf

Stephens, B. "The Tehran-Caracas Nuclear Axis." Wall Street Journal, Global View, 15/12/2009. http://online.wsj.com/article/SB100014240527487048693045745956528158027 22.html

Stone, Hannah. "FARC Using Peace Talks to Buy Arms: Ecuador General." Insight Crime Analysis, 16/01/2013. http://www.insightcrime.org/news-briefs/farc-using-peace-talks-to-buy-arms-ecuador-general

Stout, David. "Chávez Calls Bush 'the Devil' in U.N. Speech." New York Times, 20/09/2006. http://www.nytimes.com/2006/09/20/world/americas/20cnd-chavez.html?_r=0

Sulick, Michael. "Russia in Latin America: A challenge to the U.S." The Cypher Brief, 01/05/2016.
https://www.thecipherbrief.com/article/challenge-us

Suchlicki, Jaime. "Iran's influence in Venezuela: Washington should worry." The Miami Herald, 08/05/2012.
http://www.miamiherald.com/2012/08/05/2930050/irans-influence-in-venezuela-washington.html#storylink=cpy

Taboada, Hernán. "El Islam en América Latina: Del Siglo XX al XXI." Universidad Nacional Autónoma de México, otoño 2010.
http://www.revistaestudios.unc.edu.ar/articulos03/articulos/1-taboada.php

Tasch, Barbara. "China's $10 billion railway across South America is either bold or insane." Business Insider, 06/10/2015.
http://www.businessinsider.com/china-plans-to-build-a-3300-mile-railway-across-south-america-2015-6

Tegel, Simeon. "Obama and Romney forget Latin America." Global Post, 25/10/2012.
http://www.globalpost.com/dispatch/news/politics/elections/121024/latin-america-us-election-campaign-obama-romney-debate

Thompson, Ginger. "The Narco-Terror Trap." ProPublica, 12/07/2015.

https://www.propublica.org/article/the-dea-narco-terror-trap

Tovar, Ernesto J. "Guerrilla colombiana de las FARC usa armas de 27 países, informa la prensa." El Comercio, Perú, 11/01/2011.
http://elcomercio.pe/mundo/322281/noticia-guerrilla-colombiana-farc-usa-armas-27-paises-informa-prensa

Trumbull, Mark. "US-CUBA THAW: Is Obama extending economic 'lifeline' to communist regime?" The Christian Science Monitor, 12/19/2014.
http://www.csmonitor.com/USA/Foreign-Policy/2014/1219/US-Cuba-thaw-Is-Obama-extending-economic-lifeline-to-communist-regime

Vargas, Gustavo-Adolfo. "Rusia y sus relaciones con América Latina." El Nuevo Diario, 10/06/2012. http://www.elnuevodiario.com.ni/opinion/254137

Vargas Velásquez, Alejo. "Relaciones entre Estados Unidos y Latinoamérica." El Colombiano, 15/04/2012. http://www.elcolombiano.com/BancoConocimiento/R/relaciones_entre_esta dos_unidos_y_latinoamerica/relaciones_entre_estados_unidos_y_latinoameri ca.asp

Vargas, Ricardo. "The Revolutionary Armed Forces of Colombia (FARC) and the Illicit Drug Trade." Transnational Institute (TNI), 07/06/1999. http://www.tni.org/briefing/revolutionary-armed-forces-colombia-farc-and-illicit-drug-trade

Vato, Un. "Jihadists and Latin American drug traffickers merge." Borderland Beat, 05/02/2013. http://www.borderlandbeat.com/2013/02/jihadists-and-latin-american-drug.html

Warrick, Joby. "Iran accused of diplomacy offensive in US backyard." The Sydney Morning Herald, 07/01/2012. http://www.smh.com.au/world/iran-accused-of-diplomacy-offensive-in-us-backyard-20120106-1pofj.html

Warrick, Joby. "Iran seeking to expand influence in Latin America." The Washington Post, 01/01/2012. http://www.washingtonpost.com/world/national-security/iran-seeking-to-expand-influence-in-latin-america/2011/12/30/gIQArfpcUP_story.html

Weber, Jonathan. "Oil producer Venezuela is facing very rough times." Seeking Alpha, 12/25/2015. http://seekingalpha.com/article/3776736-oil-producer-venezuela-facing-rough-times

West Allen B. "Iran is a threat in Latin America." The Washington Times, 28/08/2012.http://www.washingtontimes.com/news/2012/aug/28/iran-is-a-threat-in-latin-america/

Young, Gerardo. "En EE.UU. preocupa un posible apoyo argentino al plan nuclear iraní." El Clarín, 29/10/12. http://www.clarin.com/politica/EEUU-preocupa-posible-argentino-nuclear_0_800919946.html

Zuckerman, Jessica. "Bolivia: Iran's Newest Friend in Latin America." The Foundry, 23/05/2012. http://blog.heritage.org/2012/05/23/bolivia-irans-newest-friend-in-latin-america/

PRESS & NEWS-SOURCES

ADL. "The Iranian Nuclear Threat: Why it Matters." Anti-Defamation League (ADL), 24/01/2013. http://www.adl.org/israel-international/iran/c/the-iranian-nuclear-threat-why-it-matters.html

ADN. "Nicaragua apuesta a ampliar relaciones militares." ADN, 26/06/2007. http://www.adnmundo.com/contenidos/politica/nicaragua_ejercito_relaciona s_militares_pi_260607.html

Agencia AP. "Fidel Castro revela nexos entre las Farc y Cuba." El Espectador, 14/11/2008. http://www.elespectador.com/articulo90568-fidel-castro-revela-nexos-entre-farc-y-cuba

ANSA. "Narcotráfico en América Latina, Globalización de lo Ilegal." Cinco Metas, 06/11/2009. http://www.cincometas.com/internacionales/42-info-internacional/427-narcotrafico-en-america-latina-globalizacion-de-lo-ilegal.html

Banderas News. "Mexican Cartels Buying Afghan Heroin." Banderas News, último acceso 03/07/2013. http://www.banderasnews.com/1101/nr-afghanheroin.htm

BBC. "Who are Hezbollah?" BBC News, 04/07/2010. http://news.bbc.co.uk/2/hi/middle_east/4314423.stm

BBC. "Ecuador probes President Correa 'link' to Farc rebels." BBC World, 18/05/2011. http://www.bbc.co.uk/news/world-latin-america-13436104

BBC. "Árabes y musulmanes en América Latina." BBC, Spanish, 17/03/2005. http://news.bbc.co.uk/hi/spanish/specials/newsid_4294000/4294241.stm

BBC. "Colombian Farc rebels' links to Venezuela detailed." BBC News, 19/03/2013. http://www.bbc.co.uk/news/world-latin-america-13343810

BBC. "Narcotráfico Industria Global." BBC Mundo, último acceso 03/07/2013. http://www.bbc.co.uk/spanish/extra0006drogasproduccion2.htm

BBC. "Colombia-FARC Peace Process to receive $450M in US aid." BBC, 02/05/2016.
http://www.bbc.com/news/world-latin-america-35498357

BBC. "Obama says 'days of meddling' in Latin America are past." BBC, 04/11/2015.
http://www.bbc.com/news/world-latin-america-32261550

BBC. "Iran nuclear deal: Key details." BBC, 01/16/2016.
http://www.bbc.com/news/world-middle-east-33521655

BIO. "Simón Bolívar Biography." BIO.
http://www.biography.com/people/simon-bolivar-241196

Brazil Magazine. "China Overcomes US and Becomes Brazil's Number One Trade Partner." Brazil Magazine, enero 2010.
http://www.brazzilmag.com/component/content/article/81-january-2010/11700-china-overcomes-us-and-becomes-brazils-number-one-trade-partner.html

Breitbart. "Southcom: Iran has established 80-plus cultural centers across Latin America to promote Shiite Islam." Breitbart, 03/19/2015.
http://www.breitbart.com/national-security/2015/03/19/southcom-iran-has-established-80-plus-cultural-centers-across-latin-america-to-promote-shiite-islam/

Business Insider. "The 50 most violent cities in the world." Business Insider, 01/26/2016.
http://www.businessinsider.com/most-violent-cities-in-the-world-2016-1

Canal Estrella TV. "Descubren Bases de las FARC en Panamá." Canal Estrella TV, 15/05/2012. http://www.youtube.com/watch?v=8ck7BamG0Rc

Canal RT. "Ecuador estrecha los lazos financieros con Irán pese a las sanciones occidentales." Canal RT, Actualidad, 26/08/2012.
http://actualidad.rt.com/actualidad/view/52297-ecuador-estrecha-lazos-financieros-iran-pese-sanciones-occidentales

Canal RT Actualidad. "Denuncian nexos entre las FARC y Al Qaeda." Canal RT, 09/04/2013. http://actualidad.rt.com/actualidad/view/91252-terrorista-nexos-farc-qaeda

Canal RT. "Venezuela, primer importador de armas de Latinoamérica." Canal RT Actualidad, 19/03/2013. http://actualidad.rt.com/actualidad/view/89427-venezuela-armas-sipri

Caracol TV. "Farc intercambiaron cocaína por armas con el grupo terrorista Al Qaeda: Cadena Ser." Caracol TV, 08/04/2013. http://www.caracol.com.co/noticias/internacional/farc-intercambiaron-cocaina-por-armas-con-el-grupo-terrorista-al-qaeda-cadena-ser/20130408/nota/1873870.aspx

Caza. "Fundamentalismo Islámico en América Latina." Secretos Cuba, 13/01/2009. http://secretoscuba.cultureforum.net/t11541-fundamentalismo-islamico-en-america-latina-ya-estan-aqui

Cinco Metas. "¿El narcotráfico es el futuro rector de la economía mundial?" Cinco Metas, 08/10/2009. http://www.cincometas.com/nacionales/36-modalidades/209-iel-narcotrafico-es-el-futuro-rector-de-la-economia-mundial.html

Código Venezuela. "Denuncian pacto nuclear Argentina-Venezuela-Irán." Nuevo Herald @ Código Venezuela, 13/07/2011. http://www.codigovenezuela.com/2011/07/noticias/global/denuncian-pacto-nuclear-argentina-venezuela-iran

CNN. "China's big chess move against the U.S.: Latin America." CNN Money, 03/04/2015. http://money.cnn.com/2015/03/04/news/economy/china-latin-america-relations-united-states/?iid=EL

CNN. "Iran, Hezbollah mine Latin America for revenue, recruits, analysts." CNN, 03/06/2013. http://edition.cnn.com/2013/06/03/world/americas/iran-latin-america/

CNN. "Five reasons why Venezuela may be the world's worst economy." CNN Money, 02/20/2015.
http://money.cnn.com/2015/02/20/news/economy/venezuela-economy-inflation/?iid=EL

Colombia en London. "El mundo opina sobre el proceso de paz." Colombia en London, 19/10/2012.
http://www.colombiaenlondon.com/index.php/archivo/2534-el-mundo-opina-sobre-el-proceso-de-paz

Contacto Magazine. "Fidel y Raúl Castro Vinculados al Narcotráfico." Contacto Magazine, último acceso 02/07/2013.
http://www.contactomagazine.com/narcotrafico0814.htm

Correio Braziliense. "Papa ofrece ajuda a presidente Santos no processo de paz da Colômbia." Correio Braziliense, 06/15/2015.
http://www.correiobraziliense.com.br/app/noticia/mundo/2015/06/15/intern a_mundo,486691/papa-oferece-ajuda-a-presidente-santos-no-processo-de-paz-da-colombia.shtml

EFE -. "Ahmadinejad dice que la muerte de Chávez no debilitará la relación de Irán y Latinoamérica." El País, Economía, 03/09/2013.
http://economia.elpais.com/economia/2013/03/09/agencias/1362844963_80 7630.html

EFE. "Gobiernos de China y Rusia saludan victoria de Nicolás Maduro en Venezuela." Telesur TV, 15/04/2013.
http://www.telesurtv.net/articulos/2013/04/15/Gobiernos-de-china-y-rusia-felicitan-a-nicolas-maduro-y-al-pueblo-venezolano-1497.html

EFE. "Jefe de la Policía colombiana denuncia nexos de las FARC con carteles mexicanos." América Economía, 27/04/2013.
http://www.americaeconomia.com/politica-sociedad/politica/jefe-de-la-policia-colombiana-denuncia-nexos-de-las-farc-con-carteles-mex

EFE. "Firma china construirá canal interoceánico." Siglo 21, 11/09/2012. http://www.s21.com.gt/canal-interoceanico/2012/09/11/firma-china-construira-canal-interoceanico

EFE. "Bolivia e Irán confirman su sintonía y prometen impulsar su cooperación." Agencia EFE, 11/24/2015. http://www.efe.com/efe/america/politica/bolivia-e-iran-confirman-su-sintonia-y-prometen-impulsar-cooperacion/20000035-2772517

EJU TV. "A Evo Morales: ¿Cuántas toneladas de cocaína se producen al año en Bolivia?" EJU, 08/202015. http://eju.tv/2015/08/a-evo-morales-cuantas-toneladas-de-cocaina-se-producen-al-ano-en-bolivia/

El Clarín. "Argentina y Brasil construirán un submarino nuclear." El Clarín, último acceso 03/07/2013. http://www.clarin.com/diario/2008/02/24/elpais/p-00601.htm

El Comercio. "La Crueldad de las FARC." El Comercio, Ecuador, 05/12/2011. http://www.elcomercio.com/editorial/CRUELDAD-FARC_0_602939769.html

El Comercio. "¿Cómo se convirtió Venezuela en un 'Narcoestado'?" El Comercio, Perú, 05/21/2015.
http://elcomercio.pe/mundo/latinoamerica/como-se-convirtio-venezuela-narcoestado-noticia-1812919

El Espectador. "Proceso de Paz FARC ha costado más de 14,000 millones." El Espectador, 01/17/2014. http://www.elespectador.com/noticias/paz/proceso-de-paz-farc-ha-costado-mas-de-14-mil-millones-articulo-469276

El Espectador. "El acuerdo de paz será una cuestión de meses, no de años: Santos." El Espectador, Paz, 06/09/2012. http://www.elespectador.com/noticias/paz/articulo-372920-el-acuerdo-de-paz-sera-una-cuestion-de-meses-no-de-anos-santos

El Nuevo Herald. "Relaciones Cuba Venezuela." Informe 21, 20/05/2013. http://informe21.com/relaciones-cuba-venezuela

El Nuevo Siglo. "Las Farc se arman con misiles tierra-aire." El Nuevo Siglo, 03/04/2013. http://www.elnuevosiglo.com.co/articulos/4-2013-las-farc-se-arman-con-misiles-tierra-aire.html

El País. "Las FARC y grupos vinculados con Al Qaeda intercambian cocaína por armas." El País, Política. 8/04/13. http://politica.elpais.com/politica/2013/04/08/actualidad/1365403910_47483 4.html

El País. "El papel de los mediadores para el proceso de paz en Colombia." El País, Judicial, 17/09/2012. http://www.elpais.com.co/elpais/judicial/noticias/papel-mediadores-para-proceso-paz-colombia

El Tiempo. "Farc habrían comprado 20 misiles rusos capaces de impactar naves hasta a seis kilómetros de altura." El Tiempo, Archivo, 11/07/2009. http://www.eltiempo.com/archivo/documento/CMS-5616488

El Tiempo. "Las cinco claves del acuerdo sobre justicia con las FARC." El Tiempo, 09/24/2015. http://www.eltiempo.com/politica/proceso-de-paz/acuerdo-de-justicia-de-santos-y-farc-penas-8-anos-para-autores-de-delitos-graves/16385339

El Tiempo. "Directivos de Wall Street en el Caguán." El Tiempo, 06/27/1999. http://www.eltiempo.com/archivo/documento/MAM-917182

El Universal. "En tres años se transfirieron a Cuba 18.000 millones de dólares." El Universal, 06/01/2014. http://www.eluniversal.com/nacional-y-politica/140601/en-tres-anos-se-transfirieron-a-cuba-18000-millones-de-dolares

Euractiv/AFP. "EU and Cuba sign deal to normalize ties." Euractiv.com, 03/11/2016. https://www.euractiv.com/section/global-europe/news/eu-and-cuba-sign-deal-to-normalise-ties/

DW. "End of '21st Century Socialism' in Latin America?" DW, 05/09/2013. http://www.dw.com/en/end-of-21st-century-socialism-in-latin-america/a-16800947

DW. "FARC en la lista terrorista de la UE." DW, 12/06/2002.
http://www.dw.de/farc-en-la-lista-terrorista-de-la-ue/a-575135

Fox News. "Not so fast? Lawmakers poised to fight Obama on Cuba
ambassador pick, embargo." Fox News, 07/02/2015.
http://www.foxnews.com/politics/2015/07/02/obama-pledges-new-
relationship-with-cuba-but-congress-says-not-so-fast.html

Fox News. "Republicans blast Obama restoring relations with Castro's Cuba."
Fox News, 07/02/2015.
http://www.weeklystandard.com/republicans-blast-obama-restoring-
relations-with-castros-cuba/article/982392

Harvard Square Library. "Against Nuclear Terrorism." Harvard, último acceso
02/07/2013. http://www.harvardsquarelibrary.org/hsr/Nuclear-War.php

HCV Analysis. "The OAS: Its Shameful History." Haiti-Cuba-Venezuela Analysis
(HCV), último acceso 03/07/2013.
http://hcvanalysis.wordpress.com/the-oas-its-shameful-history-parts-i-ii-and-
iii/

Iberosphere. "FARC, ETA and Al Qaeda: the terror connection." Iberosphere,
24/03/2010. http://iberosphere.com/2010/03/the-terror-connection-a-
common-cause-for-the-farc-eta-and-al-qaeda/790

InfoPuntual. "Los avances del programa nuclear argentino." Info Puntual,
02/07/2012. http://www.infopuntual.com/post/avances-programa-nuclear-
argentino-112.aspx

Infobae: "La declaración de Stiuso: A Nisman lo mató un grupo relacionado
con el gobierno anterior." INFOBAE, 03/01/2016.
http://www.infobae.com/2016/03/01/1794038-exclusivo-la-declaracion-
stiuso-a-nisman-lo-mato-un-grupo-relacionado-al-gobierno-anterior

Infobae. "Joseph Humire: El acuerdo nuclear le permite a Irán hacer más
negocios en América Latina." INFOBAE, 09/04/2015.
http://www.infobae.com/2015/09/04/1753028-joseph-humire-el-acuerdo-
nuclear-le-permite-iran-hacer-mas-negocios-america-latina

Infobae. "Brasil, Bolivia y Colombia, los blancos de Hezbollah en la región." Infobae, 17/05/2012. http://america.infobae.com/notas/50678-Brasil-Bolivia-y-Colombia-los-blancos-de-Hezbollah-en-la-regin

Infobae. "Informe de los EE.UU revela vínculos venezolanos con Irán, FARC y Hezbollah." Infobae, 21/11/2011. http://america.infobae.com/notas/38401-Informe-de-los-EEUU-revela-vinculos-venezolanos-con-Iran-las-

Insight Crime. "Impunity issue looms large over Colombia's peace process." Insight Crime, 03/03/2015. http://www.insightcrime.org/news-analysis/impunity-issue-looms-large-over-colombias-peace-process

Insight Crime. "MS13." Insight Crime. http://www.insightcrime.org/el-salvador-organized-crime-news/mara-salvatrucha-ms-13-profile

Insight Crime. "FARC-Profile." Insight Crime. http://www.insightcrime.org/colombia-organized-crime-news/farc-profile

Insight Crime. "Bolivia: The new hub for drug trafficking in South America." Insight Crime, 10/16/2014. http://www.insightcrime.org/investigations/bolivia-the-new-hub-for-drug-trafficking-in-south-america

Insight Crime. "El desafío de Evo: Bolivia, el epicentro de la droga." Insight Crime. http://es.insightcrime.org/investigaciones/el-desafio-de-evo-bolivia-el-epicentro-de-la-droga

Iran Spanish Radio. "Aumento de ventas de armas de Rusia a América Latina." Iran Spanish Radio, 03/04/2013. http://spanish.irib.ir/an%C3%A1lisis/comentarios/item/139211-aumento-de-ventas-de-armas-de-rusia-a-am%C3%A9rica-latina

La Gente Del Libro. "Islam en América Latina." YOUTUBE, 17/12/2006. http://www.youtube.com/watch?v=RSfDAEfM50Q

Latin America Current Events and News. "ISIS reportedly operating in Mexico near U.S. border." Latin America Current Events and News, 04/15/2015. http://latinamericacurrentevents.com/isis-reportedly-operating-in-mexico-near-u-s-border/34174/

La Nación. "Maduro se reunió con el Ayatolah de Irán y criticó a Estados Unidos." La Nación, 11/23/2015. http://www.lanacion.com.ar/1848094-maduro-se-reunio-con-el-ayatolah-de-iran-y-critico-a-estados-unidos

La Nación. "Nace la Celac, un nuevo bloque americano impulsado por Hugo Chávez." La Nación, 03/12/2011. http://www.lanacion.com.ar/1429832-nace-la-celac-un-nuevo-bloque-americano-sin-eeuu-ni-canada-impulsado-por-hugo-chavez

La Opinión. "FARC, Narcotráfico y Terrorismo Global." La Opinión, 09/04/2014. http://www.laopinion.com.co/farc-narcotr-fico-y-terrorismo-global-83958#ATHS

La Otra Cara. "El día en que las FARC se abrazaron con Wall Street en las selva colombiana." La Otra Cara, 08/07/2015. https://laotracara.co/nota-ciudadania/el-dia-que-las-farc-se-abrazaron-con-wall-street-en-la-selva-colombiana/

La Patilla. "¿Es Venezuela el pivote nuclear entre Argentina e Irán?" La Patilla, 09/07/2011.

http://www.lapatilla.com/site/2011/07/19/%C2%BFes-venezuela-el-pivote-nuclear-entre-argentina-e-iran-documentos-ineditos/

La República. "Sendero Luminoso se parece cada vez más a las FARC." La República Perú, 20/09/2009. http://www.larepublica.pe/21-09-2009/sendero-luminoso-se-parece-cada-vez-mas-las-farc

MercoPress. "Rusia superó a EE.UU. y es el que más armas vende a Latinoamérica." MercoPress, 06/02/2010. http://es.mercopress.com/2010/02/06/rusia-supero-a-ee.uu.-y-es-el-que-mas-armas-vende-a-latinoamerica

MercoPress. "America anticipates strong devaluation for bankrupt Venezuela." MercoPress, 02/19/2016. http://en.mercopress.com/2016/01/19/bank-of-america-anticipates-strong-devaluation-for-bankrupt-venezuela

Miami Diario. "Estados Unidos y América Latina: ¿Una relación estancada?" Miami Diario, 04/03/2013. http://www.miamidiario.com/politica/barack-obama/usa/latinoamerica/estados-unidos/voto-hispano/america-latina/reforma-migratoria/voto-latino/305585

Miami Herald. "Miami congresswoman pans 'dangerous' Colombian peace deal." Miami Herald, 03/01/2016. http://www.miamiherald.com/news/nation-world/world/article63364037.html

Miami Herald. "Radical Islam's Latin American connection." Miami Herald, 11/23/2015. http://www.miamiherald.com/opinion/op-ed/article46127140.html

Miami Herald. "Latin America: Is U.S. influence waning?" The Miami Herald, 01/05/2013. http://www.miamiherald.com/2013/05/01/3375160/latin-america-is-us-influence.html#storylink=cpy

New York Times. "The Iran Nuclear Deal – A Simple Guide." New York Times, 01/15/2015. http://www.nytimes.com/interactive/2015/03/31/world/middleeast/simple-guide-nuclear-talks-iran-us.html?_r=0

New York Times. "U.S. pushes against warnings ISIS plans to enter from Mexico." New York Times, 09/16/2014. http://www.nytimes.com/2014/09/16/us/us-pushes-back-against-warnings-that-isis-plans-to-enter-from-mexico.html

Noticias 24. "Venezuela, el Uranio y la 'conexión iraní'." Noticias 24, último acceso 03/07/2013. http://www.noticias24.com/actualidad/noticia/13079/venezuela-el-uranio-y-la-conexion-irani/

Noticierodiario.com.ar. "Hay una relación obvia de Irán con Hezbollah y de las FARC con Chávez." Noticiero Diario, 01/08/2010. http://noticierodiario.com.ar/hay-una-relacion-obvia-de-iran-con-hezbollah-y-de-las-farc-con-chavez/

Notitarde. "El modelo económico del socialismo del siglo XXI fracasó rotundamente." Notitarde, 27/04/2013. http://www.notitarde.com/Desayuno-en-la-Redaccion/El-modelo-economico-del-socialismo-del-siglo-XXI-fracaso-rotundamente-/2013/04/27/182134

NTI. "Venezuela's Search for Nuclear Power - or Nuclear Prestige." Nuclear threat initiative (NTI), last access 03/07/2013. http://www.nti.org/analysis/articles/venezuelas-search-nuclear-power/

Pensamiento Colombia. "La presencia de Hezbollah en Colombia." Pensamiento Colombia, último acceso 03/07/2013. http://www.pensamientocolombia.org/la-presencia-de-hezbollah-en-colombia

Perú 21. "EEUU: Investigan a entorno de Evo Morales por narcotráfico." Perú 21, 09/16/2015. http://peru21.pe/mundo/eeuu-investigan-entorno-evo-morales-narcotrafico-2227698

Pesos for Congress. "The Mexican Drug Cartel Joins Forces with Al Qaeda?" YouTube, 09/08/2007. http://www.youtube.com/watch?v=762PtpiBfy4

RadioJai. "La alianza entre Hezbollah, las FARC y Venezuela produce graves incidentes con la comunidad evangélica." Radio Jai, 11/01/2008. http://www.radiojai.com.ar/online/notiDetalle.asp?id_Noticia=35970

Reuters/EP. "Al Qaeda ayuda a FARC y cárteles mexicanos a introducir droga en Europa." Europa Press, 04/01/2010. http://www.europapress.es/internacional/noticia-qaeda-ayuda-farc-carteles-mexicanos-introducir-droga-europa-20100104183457.html

Reuters. "Colombia Ties Drug Ring to Hezbollah," New York Times, 22/10/2008. http://www.nytimes.com/2008/10/22/world/americas/22colombia.html?_r=0

Reuters. "Principales vínculos de Irán con Ecuador." El Universo, 09/01/2012. http://www.eluniverso.com/2012/01/09/1/1355/principales-vinculos-iran-ecuador-venezuela-nicaragua-cuba.html

Reuters. "Leader Ousted, Nation Is Now a Drug Haven." New York Times, 01/11/2012. http://www.nytimes.com/2012/11/02/world/africa/guinea-bissau-after-coup-is-drug-trafficking-haven.html?pagewanted=all&_r=0

Reuters. "Venezuela is still one of the world's most-dangerous countries." Newsweek, 02/02/2016. http://www.newsweek.com/venezuela-still-one-worlds-most-dangerous-countries-422409

Reuters. "Economías A. Latina enfrentan crecimiento modesto, decepcionante." Reuters, 07/23/2015. http://lta.reuters.com/article/topNews/idLTAKCN0PX1EQ20150723

Reuters. "Obama pledges more than $450 million aid to help Colombia peace plan." Reuters, 02/05/2016. http://www.reuters.com/article/us-usa-colombia-idUSKCN0VD2XM

Revista Cambio. "Hezbolá usa indígenas para penetrar en Latinoamérica." Revista Cambio; Colombia, 30/03/2009. http://www.cambio.com.co/paiscambio/10preguntascambio/821/ARTICULO-PRINTER_FRIENDLY-PRINTER_FRIENDLY_CAMBIO-4899911.html

Semana. "Críticos del proceso de paz... No solo es Uribe." Revista Semana, 15/09/2012. http://www.semana.com/nacion/articulo/criticos-del-proceso-paz-no-solo-uribe/264797-3

Semana. "El frente europeo de las FARC." Revista Semana, 16/02/2008. http://www.semana.com/nacion/articulo/el-frente-europeo-farc/91024-3

Semana. "The world of the FARC." Revista Semana, 05/01/2009. http://www.semana.com/print-edition/the-world-of-the-farc-part-europe/119342-3.aspx

RT News. "Obama signs law countering Iranian sway in Latin America." RT News, 12/30/2012.
https://www.rt.com/news/obama-iran-latin-america-091/

RT News. "Cooperación militar con Bolivia: Rusia se gana un socio más en América Latina." RT, 11/24/2015.
https://actualidad.rt.com/actualidad/192387-putin-rusia-dispuesta-colaborar-bolivia-campo-militar

Salon. "Is Venezuela harboring Hezbollah?" Salon, 08/01/2013.
http://www.salon.com/2013/01/08/is_venezuela_harboring_hezbollah/

Secure Empire. "Las Farc: El Mayor Cartel de Narcotráfico del Mundo." Secure Empire, último acceso 03/07/2013.
http://www.securempire.com/analisis/seguridad/geopolitica-las_farc__el_mayor_cartel_del_narcotrafico_en_el_mundo

Siglo 21. "FARC – Descubren evidencia de nexos entre las FARC y Al Qaeda." Siglo 21, último acceso 03/07/2013.
http://siglo21.com/slideshow/descubren-evidencia-de-nexos-entre-las-farc-y-al-qaeda/attachment/farc-descubren-evidencia-de-nexos-entre-la-farc-y-al-qaeda/

Sombrerodesao. "Evo Morales - Más pruebas de FRAUDE aparecen." YouTube, 16/12/2008.
http://www.youtube.com/watch?v=jRPqetitAE4&list=PLCFD5CB4CF82939C2

Spanish People. "Las FARC negociarán sin límite de tiempo." Spanish People, 11/12/2012.
http://spanish.people.com.cn/31617/8053376.html

Telesur. "Colombia: Critics skeptical of US aid for peace process." YouTube, 02/09/2016.
https://www.youtube.com/watch?v=f6jv8ow54fm

Telesur. "Europe commits to funding Colombia's peace process." Telesur, 01/19/2016.
http://www.telesurtv.net/english/news/Europe-Commits-to-Funding-Colombias-Peace-Process--20160119-0009.html

Tenacitas. "Organized crime in the Americas: What to expect in 2016."
Tenacitas, 01/15/2016.
http://www.tenacitas-intl.com/organized-crime-in-the-americas-what-to-expect-in-2016/

Testigo Directo. "Las FARC en Paraguay 3." Testigo Directo, 18/05/2010.
http://www.youtube.com/watch?v=H7722p05_3Q

Testigo Directo. "Las FARC y Al Qaeda." Testigo Directo, 08/03/2010.
http://www.youtube.com/watch?v=F0MlpkpDVR4

The Associated Press. "Venezuela, Cuba Defend Iran's Right to Have Nuclear
Program." Fox News, 21/09/2011.

http://www.foxnews.com/world/2011/09/21/venezuela-cuba-defend-irans-right-to-have-nuclear-program/#ixzz2Pj42zUp9

The Associated Press. "Secret document: Venezuela, Bolivia supplying Iran
with uranium." The Associated Press, 25/05/2009.
http://www.haaretz.com/news/secret-document-venezuela-bolivia-supplying-iran-with-uranium-1.276675

The Associated Press. "En Colombia desarticulan organización vinculada a
Hezbollah." Noticias 24, 22/10/2008.
http://www.noticias24.com/actualidad/noticia/19093/en-colombia-desarticulan-organizacion-vinculada-a-hezbollah/

The Associated Press. "Crece narcotráfico en Bolivia: ONU." Associated Press,
12/09/2011.
http://www.aztecanoticias.com.mx/notas/internacional/71453/crece-narcotrafico-en-bolivia-onu

The Daily Beast. "Iran Woos Bolivia For Influence In Latin America." The Daily
Beast, 20/05/2012. http://www.thedailybeast.com/articles/2012/05/20/iran-woos-bolivia-for-influence-in-latin-america.html

The Economist. "Brothers in arms?" The Economist, 14/01/2012.
http://www.economist.com/node/21542782

The Guardian. "Putin's Latin America trip aims to show Russia is more than just a regional power," The Guardian, 07/15/2014. http://www.theguardian.com/world/2014/jul/15/putin-latin-america-russia-power

The Guardian. "Rafael Correa." The Guardian, updated 02/07/2013. http://www.guardian.co.uk/world/rafael-correa

The Israel Project. "Iran intensifies Influence throughout Latin America." The Israel Project, last access 03/07/2013. http://www.theisraelproject.org/site/c.hsJPKOPIJpH/b.5608661/k.E577/Iran_Intensifies_Influence_throughout_Latin_America.htm

The National Interest. "Washington must remedy Colombia's flawed FARC deal." The National Interest, 02/04/2016. http://nationalinterest.org/feature/washington-must-remedy-colombias-flawed-farc-deal-15108

The News Hub. "Why Russia loves Latin America?" The News Hub, 10/06/2015. https://www.the-newshub.com/business/why-russia-loves-latin-america

"The Real Cuba"

www.therealcuba.com/

The Trumpet. "The deadly dangerous U.S.-Cuba deal." The Trumpet, March 2015.

https://www.thetrumpet.com/article/12381.24.172.0/religion/roman-catholicism/the-deadly-dangerous-us-cuba-deal

UPME. "Advierten uranio en Bolivia donde Venezuela E Irán harán planta cementera." UPME. http://www1.upme.gov.co/sala-de-prensa/noticias/advierten-uranio-en-bolivia-donde-venezuela-e-iran-haran-planta-cementera

US News. "Renewed U.S.-Cuba Ties Will Benefit Larger Relations With Latin America." US News, 12/18/2014. http://www.usnews.com/news/articles/2014/12/18/renewed-us-cuba-ties-will-benefit-relations-with-latin-america

US News. "Better economic relations with Cuba could be a win-win." US News, 12/23/2014. http://www.usnews.com/news/articles/2014/12/23/better-economic-relations-with-cuba-could-be-a-win-win

Venezuela Awareness. "Venezuela lideró la compra de armas en América Latina durante 2015." Venezuela Awareness, 02/24/2016. http://www.venezuelaawareness.com/2016/02/venezuela-lidero-la-compra-de-armas-en-america-latina-durante-2015/?utm_content=buffer4f1e3&utm_medium=social&utm_source=twitter.com&utm_campaign=buffer

Wikileaks. "Irán y Venezuela preparaban la explotación de las reservas venezolanas de uranio." Europa Press, última actualización 02/12/2010. http://www.europapress.es/latam/politica/noticia-wikileaks-iran-venezuela-preparaban-explotacion-reservas-venezolanas-uranio-20101202030557.html

World Bulletin. "U.S. names Special Envoy to Colombian peace process." World Bulletin, 02/21/2015. http://www.worldbulletin.net/colombia/155458/us-names-special-envoy-to-colombian-peace-process

World Watch Monitor. "Latin American Christians need protection from organized crime." World Watch Monitor, 09/24/2015. https://www.worldwatchmonitor.org/2015/09/4022977/

IVRepública. "Con apoyo de Rusia, Venezuela se arma hasta los dientes." YouTube, último acceso 03/07/2013. http://www.youtube.com/watch?v=z8Zs9PM-Mw0

INSTITUTIONS & GOVERNMENT

Drug Policy. "Drug Trafficking in Latin America." Drug Policy Alliance, last access 03/07/2013. http://www.drugpolicy.org/drug-trafficking-latin-america

CFR. "US-Latin America Relations." CFR Task Report, último acceso 03/07/2013. http://www.cfr.org/mexico/us-latin-america-relations/p16279

CFR. "Nuclear Terror Threat Goes 'POOF'." Council on Foreign Relations (CFR), 29/10/2012. http://www.cfr.org/weapons-of-mass-destruction/nuclear-terror-threat-goes-poof/p29363

CFR. "The global regime for transnational crime." Council on Foreign Relations, 06/25/2013.
http://www.cfr.org/transnational-crime/global-regime-transnational-crime/p28656

CFR. "FARC, ELN: Colombia's left-wing guerrillas." Council on Foreign Relations, Backgrounder.
http://www.cfr.org/colombia/farc-eln-colombias-left-wing-guerrillas/p9272

CFR. "U.S. Latin America relations." Council on Foreign Relations, May 2008.
http://www.cfr.org/mexico/us-latin-america-relations/p16279

COHA. "Russia and Latin America: Geopolitical posturing or international partnership?" Council on Hemispheric Affairs, 06/20/2014.
http://www.coha.org/russia-and-latin-america-geopolitical-posturing-or-international-partnership/

Colombia Reports. "Colombia government and FARC rebels 'agreeing to impunity' in justice deal: HRW" Colombia Reports, 12/22/2015.
http://colombiareports.com/colombia-govt-and-farc-rebels-agreeing-to-impunity-in-justice-deal/

Embajada de Rusia en Méjico. "Rusia y los Países de América Latina." Embrumex.com, último acceso 02/07/2013.
http://www.embrumex.com.mx/sp_polex_america.html

European Parliament. "Motion for a resolution on the peace process in Colombia." European Parliament, 01/11/2016. http://www.europarl.europa.eu/sides/getDoc.do?type=MOTION&reference=B 8-2016-0054&language=EN

European Union. "Federica Mogherini eyes a breakthrough in Colombia." European Union, 19/01/2016. http://eeas.europa.eu/top_stories/2016/190116_colombian-peace-process_en.htm

European Union. "EU Relations with Cuba." European Union External Action. http://eeas.europa.eu/cuba/index_en.htm

FBI. "It's not just the mafia anymore." Federal Bureau of Investigation, undated. https://www.fbi.gov/about-us/investigate/organizedcrime

Gatestone Institute. "Iran taking over Latin America." Gatestone Institute, 12/16/2015. http://www.gatestoneinstitute.org/7060/iran-latin-america

Global Initiative. "Tackling illicit links between crime and politics." Global Initiative. http://www.globalinitiative.net/the-new-criminal-powers-tackling-illicit-links-between-crime-and-politics/

Government of Iran. "Venezuela presidents call for expansion of Tehran, Caracas multilateral cooperation" Government of Iran Info, 01/10/2015. http://www.president.ir/en/83756

HRW. "Human Rights Watch's Analysis of Colombia-FARC Agreement." Human Rights Watch, 12/21/2015. https://www.hrw.org/news/2015/12/21/human-rights-watch-analysis-colombia-farc-agreement

HRW. "Colombia's compromise with murder." Human Rights Watch, 09/18/2014. https://www.hrw.org/news/2014/11/18/colombias-compromise-murder

International Peace Institute. "Milestone in Colombia peace process addresses illicit crops but not root problem." Relief Web, 06/05/2014. http://reliefweb.int/report/colombia/milestone-colombia-peace-process-addresses-illicit-crops-not-root-problem

LIT-CI. "What is XXI Century Socialism?" LIT-CI, 02/17/2007. http://litci.org/es/archive/artigo53-sp-164091585/

OPEAL. "¿Para qué sirve Unasur?" Observatorio de Política & Estrategia en América Latina (OPEAL), último acceso 03/07/2013. http://www.opeal.net/index.php?option=com_k2&view=item&id=15364:%C2%BFpara-qu%C3%A9-sirve-unasur?&Itemid=125

United Nations. "Security Council decides to establish political mission in Colombia tasked with monitoring, verifying ceasefire, cessation of hostilities." United Nations Press, 01/25/2016. http://www.un.org/press/en/2016/sc12218.doc.htm

UN General Assembly. "Thematic Debate of the 66th session of the United Nations General Assembly on Drugs and Crime as a Threat to Development." United Nations, 06/26/2012. http://www.un.org/en/ga/president/66/Issues/drugs/drugs-crime.shtml

UN News Center. "Ban hails Latin American nuclear weapon-free zone on 45th anniversary." United Nations News Center, last access 03/07/2013. http://www.un.org/apps/news/story.asp?NewsID=41239&#.UakzRtl3u8A

UNODC. "Transnational Organized Crime: The globalized illegal economy." UNODC, 2016.

https://www.unodc.org/toc/en/crimes/organized-crime.html

UNODC. "Data and Analysis." UNODC. https://www.unodc.org/unodc/en/data-and-analysis/

UNODC y Ministerio de Justicia de Colombia. "Investigación sobre Narcotráfico en Colombia." UNODC y Ministerio de Justicia, último acceso 03/07/2013. http://www.unodc.org/colombia/es/investigacionarcotrafico.html

The White House. "Transnational Organized Crime: A Growing Threat to National and International Security." The White House.
https://www.whitehouse.gov/administration/eop/nsc/transnational-crime/threat

US Congress. "China's foreign policy and ``soft power'' in South America." April, 2008.
https://www.gpo.gov/fdsys/pkg/CPRT-110SPRT41927/html/CPRT-110SPRT41927.htm

US Department of State. "U.S. Policy toward Latin America." US Department of State, 02/17/2011.
http://www.state.gov/p/wha/rls/rm/2011/156757.htm

US Department of State: Taken Question. "Argentina/Iran/Venezuela: Nuclear Technology." US Department of State, Office of the Spokesperson, 13/07/2011.
http://www.state.gov/r/pa/prs/ps/2011/07/168491.htm

US Government Interagency Working Group. "International Crime Threat Assessment." US Government, December, 2000.
http://fas.org/irp/threat/pub45270index.html

Made in United States
North Haven, CT
04 January 2022

14160240R00088